THE CHURCH

THE CHURCH,

ONE, HOLY, CATHOLIC, AND APOSTOLIC

RICHARD D. PHILLIPS, 1960-
PHILIP G. RYKEN,
AND MARK E. DEVER

P&R PUBLISHING
P.O. BOX 817 • PHILLIPSBURG • NEW JERSEY 08865-0817

Page design and typesetting by Lakeside Design Plus

Printed in the United States of America

Library of Congress Cataloging-in-Publication Data
Phillips, Richard D. (Richard Davis), 1960–
    The church : one, holy, catholic, and apostolic / Richard D. Phillips, Philip G. Ryken, and Mark E. Dever.
        p. cm.
    Includes bibliographical references and index.
    ISBN 0-87552-614-4 (pbk.)
    1. Church—Marks. 2. Church—Biblical teaching. I. Ryken, Philip Graham, 1966– II. Dever, Mark. III. Title.

BV601.P48 2004
262'.72—dc22

                                                            2004044158

*To Him who is
"head over all things to the church,
which is his body, the fullness of him who fills all in all."
—Ephesians 1:22–23*

Contents

PREFACE

The idea of the church did not fare very well in twentieth-century evangelicalism. People frequently said that they liked Jesus, but did not think too highly of the church. The church represented *religion,* a pejorative term, when what they wanted was *Christianity.* To many people, Christianity did not require the church; to some, the church was even considered a hindrance to a vibrant relationship with Christ himself. As one surveyed the evangelical press, it seemed that the most notable and most useful Christian institutions were the parachurch ministries. Therefore, many concluded, if you wanted to get serious about evangelism or missions or discipleship, you had to go around the church instead of through it.

But people are starting again to think about the church, and to think differently about her place in the Christian life. For many, this arises from a concern to realize the social dimensions of the Christian faith. Salvation, they often and rightly point out, involves more than our own individual destiny and experience. In a culture where the private and individual reign supreme, Christians want to restore the priority of public and corporate faith. Some are taking this renewed appreciation for the church to erroneous, unhealthy extremes, with not a few Christian writers seeming to discredit the individual's relationship to God altogether. But, in general, renewed interest in the church represents a healthy return to a more biblically balanced view of the Christian life, one that is more closely in sync with that of believers from ages past.

According to the Bible, the church of Jesus Christ is the preeminent institution in all this world. The church is God's gift to his children for provision, protection, and growth. The church is the vessel for the display of God's glory, not only on earth but also in the heavenly realm. To love Christ is necessarily to love his church. To be saved is to leave the world and enter into the church. Indeed, John Calvin spoke with biblical warrant when he wrote, "He who would have God for his Father must have the Church for his mother." This may sound strange to contemporary ears, but Calvin goes on to explain:

> For there is no other way to enter into life unless this mother conceive us in her womb, give us birth, nourish us at her breast, and lastly, unless she keep us under her care and guidance until, putting off mortal flesh, we become like the angels. Our weakness does not allow us to be dismissed from her school until we have been pupils all our lives . . . away from her bosom one cannot hope for any forgiveness of sins or any salvation.[1]

It was in order to encourage this renewed appreciation for the church that the Alliance of Confessing Evangelicals selected the topic "Christ and His Church" for the thirtieth anniversary meeting of the Philadelphia Conference on Reformation Theology, in April 2003. These chapters were first presented at that conference, held at Tenth Presbyterian Church in downtown Philadelphia. Our approach was to examine the church through the lens provided by the first great ecumenical confession, the Nicene Creed, dating in its present form from A.D. 381. Our fathers in the faith described the church as "one, holy, catholic, and apostolic," and it is the authors' contention that as the church recovers the character enshrined in these words, she may better realize her calling in our world today.

The authors wish to thank our friends and colleagues associated with the Alliance of Confessing Evangelicals, and to express our gratitude to Allan Fisher of P&R Publishing for his interest in printing this material. We offer these studies with thanks to God for Christ and his church, and with a desire that the reader may learn more to love Christ by loving the church, better to serve Christ by serving his church, and more clearly to know the union we have with Christ through fellowship with his one, holy, catholic, and apostolic church. "To God be glory in the church and in Christ Jesus throughout all generations, forever and ever. Amen."

1

PROLOGUE: "I WILL BUILD MY CHURCH"

MATTHEW 16:13–25

RICHARD D. PHILLIPS

He said to them, "But who do you say that I am?"
Simon Peter replied, "You are the Christ, the Son
of the living God." And Jesus answered him, "Blessed
are you, Simon Bar-Jonah! For flesh and blood has
not revealed this to you, but my Father who
is in heaven." —Matthew 16:15–17

---

*I*f you really want to understand something, one of the best things you can do is study its origin, or beginning. This is true of nations. If you want to understand why America is as it is today, what its institutions are about, how its identity was formed, then you have to go back to learn about its birth in the Revolu-

1

tionary War, its struggle as a colony seeking independence, its ideal of equality under God, its pursuit of life, liberty, and happiness.

The same is true of sports and pastimes. I recently took time to investigate the invention of my favorite sport, football. Its roots begin in the English game of rugby. The great Walter Camp, captain of the Yale University team, introduced rule changes in the 1880s that transformed the sport to what we know and love today. He introduced the play from scrimmage, the point differential between touchdowns and field goals, set plays, and the eleven-man limit of players on the field. In 1906, when the game was bogging down in mass brutality, he brought the innovation of the forward pass. Camp's goal was to take English rugby's virtues of physical strength and stamina and combine them with the American virtues of speed, daring, imagination, and strategy. These are the very things that explain the vital connection between football and the American ethos.

That same approach of searching out origins yields benefits when studying religions. If you want to understand the heart and soul of the English Reformed churches, you must reckon with the flames lit by the Roman Catholic queen, "Bloody" Mary, wherein they received their true birth. If you want to know what lies at the heart of Islam, you must consider its founder, Mohammed, and its first century of expansion carved out by the sword. And, of course, if you want to really lay hold of the heart of the Christian church as a whole, to understand its values and aspirations and guiding principles, you must go back to the New Testament record of Jesus Christ's ministry.

The Origins of the Christian Church

In a very real way the origins of the church may be traced to the events recorded in Matthew 16. Matthew bears witness to a pivotal point in the ministry of our Lord. After his baptism and temptation, Jesus came to Galilee, where he taught of God's kingdom, demonstrated its reality through his miracles, and gathered his disciples around himself. Matthew chapters 4–15 record this stage of his ministry. The miracle of feeding the multitudes with only a few pieces of bread, the only miracle recorded in all four Gospels, culminates this phase with a dramatic presentation of Jesus as leader of the new exodus, as the true Passover Lamb, and as the Messiah who feeds his pilgrim people with manna from heaven. This is what the Galilean ministry pointed to: the gathering of the church in the wilderness for the exodus to the Promised Land, with the new Moses in its vanguard.

Matthew 16 follows this with the Pharisees' opposition to our Lord. By and large, that was the result of Jesus' Galilean ministry: he was rejected by all but a handful of disciples. Jesus thus withdrew with the Twelve, but not in defeat. Here is the origin of the Christian church— the twelve disciples, separated from the leaven of unbelief, walking with Jesus through a barren land.

It is noteworthy that this passage (Matt. 16:13–25) begins by telling us where Jesus took his protochurch. "Jesus came," Matthew records, "into the district of Caesarea Philippi." This center of Graeco-Roman culture in Palestine had a large pagan population. Indeed, it would have been hard to find a place more symbolic of the whole system of the world's idolatry. The city boasted a famous cave that housed an ancient shrine to Baal, but that the Greeks had dedicated to their god Pan. The region is thus known in some ancient literature as Paneas. Archaeologists have informed us that the region was filled with temples to various Greek gods. Furthermore, the tetrarch Philip, in order to ingratiate himself with Augustus Caesar, had erected a temple, resplendent in white marble, massive in size, and dedicated to the worship of the Roman emperor, and renamed the place Caesarea Philippi. The idolatries of the seductive Orient, of philosophical Greece, and of militant Rome coalesced in this center of pagan religion. One writer says, "It is as if most of the rivulets of various ancient religions converged here."[1] It was to this place, having proclaimed his kingdom in Galilee, that Jesus brought his little remnant church.

We are talking about the origin of the Christian church, and we can make some observations already. Jesus, having proclaimed his kingdom to Israel and been rejected, having claimed and gathered the small band of his church to himself, now faces them outward toward the world. Note that the church, being formed in this fledgling band, does not turn towards the past, inward toward the exclusive world of Judaism, but toward the future, outward toward the Gentile world that Jesus is going to include within his saving realm. Also notice that when Jesus brings his disciples to the place where he is going to challenge them to believe on him, he brings them before the idols of this world. Often faith must be professed in awareness of and in the presence of the false idols. For to profess that Jesus Christ is Lord is also to reject the idolatry that is offered by the world. Michael Green helpfully observes:

> Today, when the world is a global village, and when the multiplicity of faiths is regarded as a fatal objection to the Christian claim of the uniqueness of Jesus, it is easy to forget that the seductions of syncretism in religion were every bit as attractive in the world where Christianity was born, and they were steadily and consistently resisted. Millions died for their quiet conviction that in the world of the relative the Absolute had arrived. Christianity cannot renege on that claim without a total denial of her Lord.[2]

The first thing Jesus insists upon, at the very moment of the church's origination, is the claim that he alone is Lord.

A Great Profession

With that introduction in mind, we may proceed into the body of this account, where we survey the origins of the Christian church in four points: *a great profession, a great promise, a great prophecy,* and *a great principle.*

First is the great profession of faith for which our Lord brought his disciples to this place. Matthew tells us that "when Jesus came into the district of Caesarea Philippi, he asked his disciples, 'Who do people say that the Son of Man is?'" (Matt. 16:13). That was the issue then, just as it is today. At the center of our belief is not what we believe about various philosophical or theological perspectives. It always comes back to the person and work of Jesus Christ. It is on him that the church rests, and it is on the answer to this question that the church stands or falls.

Naturally, there were a number of points of view. "They said, 'Some say John the Baptist, others say Elijah, and others Jeremiah or one of the prophets'" (v. 14). This is just as it is today—people have differing views about what we should make of Jesus. Jesus therefore focused his attack, demanding, "But who do you say that I am?" (v. 15). When studying the church, we inevitably emphasize our corporate union in Christ, but it is right to remember at the outset that salvation always begins with the individual standing before Jesus, who demands a personal reckoning with who and what he is.

If you were to put your finger on the single verse that forms the very center of Matthew's Gospel—or of any of the three Synoptic Gospels—the fulcrum on which this great gospel record balances, that verse would have to be Matthew 16:16. It is a verse all Christians should know. Prior to this, Jesus has been calling people to himself with the aim of founding his church. But as soon as this conversation takes place, Jesus rejoices because what happens in this verse both begins the church and ensures its ultimate triumph.

From this verse forward, Jesus' public ministry is over. Matthew 16 records the origin of the Christian church; its founding takes place in this interaction between Jesus and the disciples and in the teaching that follows. After these events, Jesus gathers up his little church and makes a beeline for the cross (Matt. 16:21–17:13). Luke records the transition by saying that Jesus, immediately after this sequence, "set his face to go to Jerusalem" (Luke 9:51). What happens in this encounter, centered on Matthew 16:16, serves as the dividing line between Jesus' public ministry of calling sinners to himself and the private ministry of training the disciples, even as he began the journey to Jerusalem and the cross.

What, then, happened in this great verse, Matthew 16:16? Did some political leader announce a new program of peace and prosperity? Was a major battle fought on some hardened plain? Did a scientist make a startling discovery? No, it was nothing that gained the world's attention. What happened then matters most even today—it has the greatest eternal significance and is of greatest concern to God. A simple man called by Jesus Christ made a profession of faith in his name.

"Who do you say that I am?" Jesus demanded. Simon Peter replied, "You are the Christ, the Son of the living God." That is what we call "the Great Confession." It is great both because of the occasion (the first formal profession of faith that is accepted as such by our Lord) and also because of its content (which is just as great today when any sinner professes who Jesus is).

Peter's great profession consists of two elements. First, it deals with Jesus' office and work. Peter calls Jesus "the Christ," that is, "the Messiah." This comes from the Hebrew verb meaning "to anoint." The Messiah is "the Anointed One." Michael Green summarizes:

> In Judaism it meant the one who would come and fulfill the hopes of the nation. Traditionally, three sorts of people had been anointed with oil: prophets, priests and kings. And Jesus in fact did fulfill the expectations of all

7

those three roles. Like the priest (only perfectly) he put people in touch with God. Like the prophet (only perfectly) he showed people what God was like. And like the king (only perfectly) he exercised God's rule over God's people while himself being uniquely the Servant of the Lord.[3]

Peter professes his faith that Jesus is the One anticipated by the whole Old Testament to bring the full-orbed salvation that was the hope of Israel. Jesus is the Christ: prophet, priest, and king.

The second part of Peter's great profession deals with the person of Christ. "You are the Son of the living God," he said. The Bible calls us to believe as Peter did about Jesus Christ; on Peter's profession the church is built. It is not enough to consider Jesus a sublime guru or even the most exemplary of all men. Matthew's Gospel records the voice of God, audible from heaven, on two occasions—Jesus' baptism, which inaugurated his public ministry, and Jesus' transfiguration, which concluded it at the church's founding—repeating exactly: "This is my beloved Son" (Matt. 3:17; 17:5). We must therefore receive him in this way, not just following him as the best of men but worshiping him as the only true God. We must profess him the way doubting Thomas eventually did: "My Lord and my God!" (John 20:28)

This is the great profession, which serves as the ground upon which each of us must be saved and upon which Jesus builds his church. Jesus is the Christ—the Messiah and Savior—and he is the Son of God. The apostle John later wrote his entire Gospel with the aim of bringing us to these two vital points of faith: "These are written so that you may believe that Jesus is the Christ, the Son of God, and that by believing you may have life in his name" (John 20:31).

We cannot place too much emphasis on this profession or on its centrality to the Christian church. We should notice, then, the very significant comment Jesus made immediately upon receiving it. He said, "Blessed are you, Simon Bar-Jonah! For flesh and blood has not revealed this to you, but my Father who is in heaven" (Matt. 16:17).

The great profession stands at the center of a saving relationship to Christ. What is it, then, that produces this profession of faith? Jesus says that it comes not by flesh and blood but by revelation from God. By "flesh and blood," he refers to all the avenues of human exploration and attainment. Peter did not come by this faith through scholarship or by philosophical inquiry. It did not spring forth from conventional wisdom or his common sense appreciation of things picked up as a fisherman. It was not something he worked out on his own even through his extensive personal experience with Jesus and his eyewitness participation in the great miracles. His great profession did not come by flesh and blood, "but by my Father who is in heaven," Jesus said. The key word here is "revealed." Peter's faith arose from the revelation of God the Father. I do not think that Jesus meant that Peter had some sudden or hidden illumination directly from God, but rather that this revelation came from Jesus himself, who is the living Word. That is where the first profession of faith came from, and that is where it comes from still—God's revelation through his Word, centered on Jesus Christ.

If that is true, and if the origination of the church tells us about how the church continues to be built today, then this tells us something of great significance. If we want people to join in Peter's great profession and thus to be admitted into the saving company of Christ's people, then we must not rely on flesh and blood devices. We must not be tempted by the things that appeal to men and women today, especially the entertainment that so dominates our secular culture and, sadly, much of the church as well. We may make the most effective appeals to flesh and blood, to the things that are persuasive and enticing to the fleshly nature of mankind. But Jesus here assures us that by those means we will never bring about the saving faith first professed by Simon Peter. Instead, we must rely on the one means God has provided: his Word. As we teach and proclaim God's Word about Jesus, the Father in heaven reveals the truth to the minds and hearts of men and brings them to true and saving faith.

A Great Promise

Simon Peter's profession was so great, and so important to our Lord, that Jesus responded with a great promise: "I tell you, you are Peter, and on this rock I will build my church" (Matt. 16:18).

This promise has been co-opted by the Roman Catholic Church to argue that Jesus was promising its exclusivity as his church upon the earth. Let me briefly explain why we can be absolutely sure that this is not what Jesus intended. First, even if we agree that Jesus is speaking of Peter himself as "the rock" on which he will build his church—and there is a sense in which we are bound to say that he is—this does not connect with the idea of papal supremacy.

Rome teaches that since Peter was the first bishop of Rome, and since Jesus promised to build his church on Peter, then the Roman Catholic Church is the one true church, and the succeeding bishops of Rome, the popes, maintain his supreme standing in the church. But there are gaping holes in this argument. If we were to point to a specific church that Peter founded, it would be the one in Jerusalem, not to mention the one in Antioch, both of which went on to become patriarchal sees in the early church. One church we can be sure Peter did not found is the one in Rome. The Book of Acts tells us that there were men from Rome who came to faith on that first Pentecost (Acts 2:10); undoubtedly, these men returned home and began the church in that city. Any relationship Rome might have to Peter as founder of its church, namely that Peter preached the Pentecost sermon, is the same relationship every other church had to Peter. Later on, when Paul wrote his crucial letter to the Romans, neither he nor Peter had yet been there, and there was a thriving church in the place. If Peter ended up in Rome and died there, as tradition strongly insists, that does not place any distinctive stamp on his relationship to the Roman church in contrast with any of the others.

Furthermore, there is by definition no such thing as apostolic succession. Paul says that the apostles labored to build the foundation of the church (Eph. 2:20). This "house-model" for the historical building of the church is very insightful. Once a foundation is laid, you do not go on building it; instead you build the house on it. Similarly, the apostles labored for the once-for-all founding of the church, and when that was done their office was discontinued. Acts makes clear that one of the requirements for being an apostle is that you had to have personally witnessed the risen Lord Jesus Christ (Acts 1:22); by biblical definition, then, no one today or at any time since that initial church age is able to fulfill the requirements of being an apostle.

With the Roman falsehood cleared away we may now look seriously at Jesus' word play: "You are Peter" (which in Greek is *petros*), "and on this Rock" (the Greek word *petra*) "I will build my church." It is useless to deny that in some sense our Lord is speaking about Peter personally. In what sense he speaks becomes clear. First, Jesus is speaking of Peter *inasmuch as he is professing saving faith*. "The rock is not just Peter, but Peter *in his confessional capacity* . . . The point is this: Jesus had found in Peter a real believer, and on that foundation he could build his church."[4] This becomes all too clear when Jesus goes on to speak of his impending crucifixion. Peter was horrified by such a thought; his vision of Christ's church had nothing to do with the cross (in this, we may consider him the first modern evangelical!). What then happened? Did Jesus say, "Well, okay, since after all you are Peter, and I have just said that your interpretation of my Word is going to have to be authoritative"? Quite the opposite—Jesus exclaimed to Peter, "Get behind me, Satan! You are a hindrance to me" (Matt. 16:23). Peter is a solid rock for Jesus' building of the church only as he himself stands fast upon the great profession of faith.

Second, Peter is singled out here as he represents the apostles as a group, and as his witness represents their collective teaching that is set down in the New Testament.

In other words, Jesus is asserting here the apostolicity of the church, represented by Peter. Peter is the one who would lead the Twelve in the weeks after Jesus' death and resurrection; it is he who would preach that great founding sermon on the first Pentecost.

Jesus said to Peter, "I will give you the keys of the kingdom of heaven, and whatever you bind on earth shall be bound in heaven, and whatever you loose on earth shall be loosed in heaven" (Matt. 16:19). It is on this basis that Roman Catholics speak of Peter as the doorman at the gates of heaven, and also on which the pope presumes to sell indulgences granting forgiveness of sins. But we should observe that just two chapters later, Jesus grants this authority to the apostles as a whole (Matt. 18:18). Indeed, we should see this authority passed down to the teaching and ruling office of the church even today in its declarative authority and in the exercise of church discipline. We do not grant forgiveness, but declare it in keeping with Christ's teaching in Scripture; this is the authority granted to the apostles and passed on to all faithful ministers. To be sure, Peter was later a man to be reckoned with in the church, as Ananaias and Sapphira discovered. But the same could be said of all the apostles, just as it should be said of faithful ministers in the church today.

Third, Jesus' meaning is clearly revealed in the choice of words he uses for his word play about Simon Peter. He said, "You are Peter," using the Greek word *petros,* meaning "rock" or "stone." He then added, "and on this rock I will build my church," using a different word, *petra,* which means not "stone" but "bedrock." The point is obvious: Peter (*petros*) is a rock

13

representative of and part of the bedrock (*petra*) of saving faith. It is the latter on which Jesus will build his church. Peter is distinctive as the first to profess that faith. When Peter stops or fails to believe (Matt. 16:23), he is no longer part of that bedrock of faith. Jesus says to the same Peter in his unbelief, "Get behind me, Satan! You are a hindrance to me."

Jesus speaks, then, of Peter as a man who makes true profession of faith in him as Christ and Son of God, and he also sees in Peter the apostolic office in the church that he will head. Upon this solid rock—all of it resting itself upon the bedrock of the faith revealed in God's Word—Jesus makes the great promise, "I will build my church."

This should not be taken as a mere statement of intent; rather, it is a divine promise. On the great profession of faith—as originally spoken by Peter and as spoken by all true believers today—Jesus will build his church. He does not assign this promise to the church growth programs that seek to build on things other than the great profession. But he speaks to every struggling pastor trying to teach unwilling people in difficult settings, and to every young Christian filled with zeal and seeking to make a difference for Christ, and to every body of elders trying to redirect their church body in a biblical way, that if only we will teach God's Word, by which God reveals to sinful men and women the great profession of faith in his Son, Jesus Christ, Jesus promises that he will build his church.

He did not promise to build great financial enterprises. He did not promise to make the minister famous or popular. He did not promise media empires or vast buildings like the temple to Caesar just ahead on the distant hilltop in Caesaria Philippi. He promised to build his church, the true people of God called out from the world to follow Jesus Christ and find their salvation in him.

A Great Prophecy

Jesus added to this great promise an equally great prophecy. He said, "I will build my church, and the gates of hell shall not prevail against it" (Matt. 16:18).

We tend to think of this in a defensive manner: no matter what attacks the devil unleashes on the church, the church will always prevail. That, of course, is true. I think, in this regard, of the great intellectual assaults made against the Christian faith over the past several centuries. Probably no one has better represented this attack than the French atheist Voltaire, whose writings were so popular during the Enlightenment.

Voltaire wrote that in fifty years from his time no one would remember Christianity. "In twenty years," he boasted, "Christianity will be no more. My single hand shall destroy the edifice it took twelve apostles to rear." But twenty years passed and Christianity remained. Voltaire, however, died, and in death even he remembered Christianity. The doctor who attended him records that his last words were these: "I am abandoned by God and man! I will give you half of what I am worth if you will give me six months' life. Then I shall go to hell; and you will go with me. O Christ! O Jesus Christ!" Fifty years came after Voltaire's famous boast, and the house from which he assaulted Christ's church with his pen was by then the headquarters of the Geneva Bible Society, from which the church was mass-producing and disseminating Bibles.[5]

Such it has always been with hell's assault on the church by means of the pen. What about the sword? I was greatly inspired by a recent account of the suffering church in the Sudan. One of the war-torn villages there is Chali, which was also one of the first missionary stations in that country and from which the Uduk tribe was converted to Christianity. In 1996 forces of the Islamic national government attacked Chali. The church was blown apart; Bibles were gleefully torn up, the pages used to roll cigarettes. Most of the men were killed immediately, some crucified, while the women were taken and abused. All of this was because of their faith in Christ. Does that raise a question as to Christ's prophecy when the church is faced with the sword? The Uduks themselves have not doubted the word of their Lord. When rebels recaptured Chali several years ago, the Christians returned and the first thing they rebuilt was their church. The gates of hell did not prevail against it. There they still gather daily to pray and worship God. Of God's sufficiency for them, their pastor, Simon Mamud, remarked, "We have nothing, but we have everything."[6]

Jesus prophesied that his church will stand against the devil and against hades. And yet we really should understand this prophecy not merely in the negative sense but also in the positive. When Jesus speaks of the "gates of hell," it is clear that he is talking about his church on the offensive, breaking down the devil's strongholds. Is this not a truth that is demonstrated in the whole Bible? Moses showed up in Egypt with only a staff, but by the power of God he broke the strength and will of Pharaoh.

Israel arrived in laughable weakness before the high walls of Jericho, but through their obedience to God and by his might those walls came crashing down. So it was for David in his great triumph over the giant Goliath, and for Hezekiah when he prayed and the angel of the Lord struck down tens of thousands in the Assyrian camp, and for Esther when her prayers were answered and her courage bore fruit as wicked Haman swung from the gibbet he had erected for faithful Mordecai.

So it was when Jesus Christ took up the cross and embraced to his own breast the very death our sins deserved. There, Satan bruised Jesus' heel, as God had foretold. But Jesus crushed Satan's head by conquering death through his own unconquerable life, by overthrowing Satan's rule like a strong man who breaks into a house to set the captives free, and by dying in the place of sinners so that we might be freed forever from the guilt of sin and delivered from its power through the working of the Holy Spirit Jesus sends into our lives. In Christ, even death—that gateway to hades—shall not prevail against us; Christ has removed death's sting for us and made it a portal to glory.

"On this rock," Jesus cried, standing before the assembled gods of this present evil age and speaking of the faith God reveals to his own people, "I will build my church, and the gates of hell shall not prevail against it." That is a prophecy, and it is found to be true whenever Christian people and churches take their stand upon God's Word so that others come to faith and the church is built up and the kingdom of God advances victoriously against the broken ranks of the devil.

A Great Principle

This leads to my fourth and last point, which is the great principle that Jesus insists upon as inseparable from everything that has happened and has been said in this pivotal encounter. This great principle is presented to us immediately following Peter's great profession. Matthew writes, "From that time Jesus began to show his disciples that he must go to Jerusalem and suffer many things from the elders and chief priests and scribes, and be killed, and on the third day be raised" (Matt. 16:21). The great principle Jesus set forth is that the great profession and the great promise and the great prophecy are all inseparably linked to his own death on the cross. Jesus meant not merely that the cross was itself the event that made all this possible—though that certainly is true—but that the cross is the way and the pattern for everything he had said and promised would come to pass. "If anyone would come after me," Jesus concludes, "let him deny himself and take up his cross and follow me" (v. 24).

This is the principle that must govern Christ's church, namely, that his power is that which comes from God through the cross. The cross must be our profession, but it also defines our discipleship. "Whoever would save his life will lose it," Jesus explained, "but whoever loses his life for my sake will find it" (v. 25). The cross is the weapon by which the church invincibly advances, for by it sin is put away, and with it death and condemnation.

This is what Paul would so ferociously insist upon in that momentous era when Christ began to build his church throughout the ancient world. People wanted a message different from the one Paul preached, but he insisted, "Jews demand signs and Greeks seek wisdom, but we preach Christ crucified" (1 Cor. 1:22–23). To the Galatians, who like so many today wanted to extend the church on the basis of worldly wisdom and achievement, Paul asserted, "Far be it from me to boast except in the cross of our Lord Jesus Christ, by which the world has been crucified to me, and I to the world" (Gal. 6:14). The cross is the great principle by which we are held fast to the great profession, to the great promise of our Lord, and to his prophecy of triumph for the church.

"Be of Good Cheer, Brother Ridley"

I said at the beginning that we really learn about something by going back to its origins. One example I gave was that of the English Protestant tradition, a lineage from which most American evangelicals have sprung, including me. If we are Baptist or Presbyterian, Methodist or Episcopalian, to name just the better-known denominations, we gather as churches that found a distinct starting place in the great English Reformation of the sixteenth century. What went on then therefore says quite a lot about why we are gathered here now.

The English Reformation drew its impetus from the reforming cry of John Wycliffe, then from the translation of the Bible into English by William Tyndale, and also from the writings of Martin Luther as they crossed over the English Channel. But its formal beginning arose from Henry VIII's desire to divorce his wife, Catherine of Aragon, who had failed to produce a male heir. In order to achieve his desire, Henry had to break free from the pope, creating the Church of England.

During Henry's reign, and especially during the short reign of his Protestant son, Edward VI, a great many courageous Christians sought to advance the cause of biblical religion in England. When they had power, they used it to enforce their reforms. They seized the Catholic monasteries (whose wealth passed largely into the hands of Protestant lords), and wielding the sword, they removed what they regarded as Catholic superstitions and blasphemies. The illiterate priests were placed under the authority of the reforming Archbishop Cranmer and his firebrand bishops—men like Hooper and Latimer and Bradford. By these means, biblical religion was spread with great thoroughness throughout England.

But, as it is said, those who live by the sword die by the sword. So it was for the English Reformers. Young King Edward died prematurely, and his elder sister, Catherine of Aragon's daughter, Mary, ascended the throne. The Catholic bishops came back, the mass was restored, and the Reformation was overthrown at a stroke.

Soon, there was a price to be paid by those who led the Reformation, and the reign of fire that earned Mary the nickname "Bloody" was soon begun. First among the Protestant clergy were two of the leading Reformers, the bishop Hugh Latimer and the London preacher Nicholas Ridley. Mary condemned them to be burned at the stake for their heresy against Roman Catholicism.

When the day of reckoning came, people gathered round to see how stalwart these leaders would be now that they no longer had the power of the state backing up their sermons. Ridley was brought out first and when he reached the stake he lifted up his face and hands toward heaven. Seeing Latimer, who now arrived, he embraced and kissed him, saying, "Be of good cheer, brother, for God will either assuage the fury of the flames, or else strengthen us to abide it."[7] Ridley then knelt by his stake, kissed it, and prayed, while Latimer knelt, also praying to God. After a Catholic priest harangued them regarding the doctrine of transubstantiation, the rejection of which was the formal cause of their burning, they were chained tightly to their stake.

As the flames kindled at Ridley's feet, Latimer spoke the words that have blazed brightly through Christian history: "Be of good cheer, Brother Ridley, and play the man; we shall this day light such a candle, by God's grace, in England, as I trust never shall be put out." Ridley then prayed, "Heavenly Father, I give Thee most hearty thanks that Thou has called me to a profession of Thee even unto death. I beseech Thee, Lord God, have mercy on this realm of England, and deliver the same from all her enemies."[8] Then, crying out for God to receive their spirits, the two men of God were consumed by the flames before the assembled crowd.

That is just a small sample of the courageous, joyous, biblically clear testimony of scores of Protestant leaders. What they unsuccessfully tried to press upon England in their days of power, they permanently emblazoned in the peoples' hearts in their days of martyrdom.

Here is the point, the principle Jesus insisted on when Peter tried to rebuke him for speaking of his cross. If we want to be a church armed with the might of God, then we must not rely upon the worldly power of men—all the more when it is available for our use. "Some trust in chariots and some in horses," says the psalmist, "but we trust in the name of the LORD our God" (Ps. 20:7). It is not by raising money or erecting crystal cathedrals or accumulating political or media power that Christ's church finds its power. "I want to know Christ," Paul said, "and the power of his resurrection and the fellowship of sharing in his sufferings, become like him in his death, and so, somehow, to attain to the resurrection from the dead" (Phil. 3:10–11 NIV).

It is when Christian men and women take their stand on God's Word before the watching world, living in holiness and ready to suffer for the sake of our Lord, that our church today will have the power of God that is able to cast down strongholds and crash open the gates of hell. It is when we take seriously the cross of Jesus Christ and its claims upon our lives that the world will stand up and take notice. It is when our message is not the easy, breezy, self-centered spirituality so common today, but Christ crucified, and a cross-bearing life for those who follow him to glory—it is then that the light of the open tomb will flood our church with the power of God. *Then* Christ will build his church in our midst and cast down even the gates of hell, all to the praise of the glory of his name.

> Here we have a firm foundation,
> here the refuge of the lost;
> Christ's the Rock of our salvation,
> his the name of which we boast.
> Lamb of God, for sinners wounded,
> sacrifice to cancel guilt!
> None shall ever be confounded
> who on him their hope have built.[9]

2

ONE CHURCH

EPHESIANS 4:1–6

RICHARD D. PHILLIPS

*I therefore, a prisoner for the Lord, urge you to walk in
a manner worthy of the calling to which you have been
called, with all humility and gentleness, with patience,
bearing with one another in love, eager to maintain the
unity of the Spirit in the bond of peace. There is one
body and one Spirit—just as you were called to the one
hope that belongs to your call—one Lord, one faith,
one baptism, one God and Father of all, who is over all
and through all and in all. —Ephesians 4:1–6*

O n May 17, 2000, George Carey, Archbishop of
Canterbury and head of the worldwide Anglican Communion, preached at ecumenical vespers in Toronto, Canada, with a Roman Catholic cardi-
nal at his side. He informed his listeners that "for the first
time, Anglican and Roman Catholic leaders from around
the world are meeting together in order to discuss the prob-

23

lems and challenges that lie before us on the road to the full visible unity of our two Churches." Immediately upon making that statement, Carey noted that many critics would charge that this represented an abandonment of Reformation principles and the gospel faith. To this he replied, "Polemics lead to hatred and division." He spoke with satisfaction of having joined Pope John Paul II for the ceremony of opening the Holy Door at St. Paul's in Rome for the beginning of the millennial jubilee year, wearing on his finger the Episcopal ring given by an earlier pope to one of his predecessors as Archbishop of Canterbury.

An Eastern Orthodox leader in attendance explained, "The Church is one, and there is only one Church of Christ. For the Church is his body. And Christ is never divided." Carey comments,

> The crisis of Christian division is the sad legacy of the past and our continuing failure to heal it. Although we personally are not to blame for those historical circumstances which have lead to today's divided Church we are accountable to the degree that we are unwilling to work for resolution of the results of past conflicts.

One reads this sermon and recalls that the church over which Carey was head was born in the flames of Smithfield, where the founders of the Anglican Church were burned to death rather than accept union with the Roman Catholic Church and its unbiblical doctrines. An optimistic reader might conclude that Carey had succeeded in winning doctrinal agreement with Rome, that the pope now embraced doctrines like salvation through faith alone and *sola scriptura,* and had repudiated the doctrine of transubstantiation (the actual doctrine over which many Anglican founders gave their lives). However, Carey did not announce accord in matters of truth; instead he announced that for Christians like his Anglican fore-bearers to divide over doctrine is un-Christ-like. He justified this view from Ephesians, pointing out that the Apostle Paul wrote, "With all humility and gentleness, with patience, bear with one another in love, making every effort to maintain a unity of the spirit and the bond of peace" (Eph. 4:2–6).[1]

The "Problem" of Christian Division

It is hard sometimes to deny that God has a sense of humor, and Carey's visit to Rome provides a choice example. The archbishop, the pope, and a representative of Eastern Orthodoxy stood together at the Holy Door of St. Peter's at the dawn of the new millennium. With the collective breath of a great throng standing by, each grasped a handle to open a new era together, but when they pulled, the door would not open. Someone, it seems, had forgotten to oil the hinges! That is, I think, a very fine metaphor for the problem of church unity without agreement in the truth. However hard you may try, such a door simply will not open. Carey, of course, saw this episode differently. For with a great deal of effort and with multitudes watching in anguish, the three not-very-athletic figures managed to pry the door open. Carey saw this as a metaphor for the ecumenical labor needed to achieve Christian union and thus as an example to us all.

Despite the various unoiled doors that constantly foil attempts at outward unity among Christians, we hear today a constant cry against the "problem" of Christian division. Roman Catholic apologists use this as one of their main arguments against the Reformation and its doctrine of Scripture alone. One group argues, "Today there are tens of thousands of competing denominations, each insisting its interpretation of the Bible is the correct one. The resulting divisions have caused untold confusion among millions of sincere but misled Christians."[2] Catholics and Protestants who bemoan this problem point to Jesus' prayer as proof that visible unity should be our top priority. Jesus prayed, asking "that they may all be one" (John 17:21).

What are we to make of this matter? I think the best answer, and the one Paul gives in our passage, is not to solve the problem of Christian unity but to deny its existence. Let me state that again: according to Paul the church is already united. He says, "There is one body and one Spirit" (Eph. 4:4). Not that there *ought to be* one body, but that there *is* one body, one unified church. We are not exhorted to "create" unity among Christians, but to maintain it, that is, to serve and promote the unity that is already a fact (Eph. 4:3). Likewise, Jesus prayed to the Father, not to us, for church unity, and we can be sure that his prayer was answered. This was the assertion of the Nicene Creed, the formula of which shapes our treatment of the church in this book. There is "one, holy, catholic, and apostolic church." There is no problem of unity in Christ's church, for it is already one.

Many will point to the existence of the various denominations and their disagreements. This is what

Roman Catholics do, arguing that apart from the pope's headship the church is fragmented. Several years ago this was asked in a question to *Christianity Today* magazine, and the editor, Bruce Shelley, answered the question quite ably. He wrote, "Denominations were created . . . to make unity in the church possible." He explained, "Considering the human inability always to see the truth clearly, differences of opinion about the outward form of the church are inevitable."[3] Denominations allow us to have organizational unity where we have full agreement, and allow us to have spiritual unity with other denominations, since we are not forced to argue our way to perfect agreement but can accept our differences of opinion on secondary matters.

A few years ago I received a call from the new pastor of a notoriously liberal church not far from where I was pastoring. It turned out that the man was an evangelical, and he wanted fellowship and advice on introducing biblical faith to his congregation. Because we were not in the same denomination, we could have unity in the gospel. We didn't have to argue about the mode of baptism or sundry other issues, and during his ministry he received loving brotherhood from our whole pastoral staff. I once even filled his pulpit when he became sick. We had a spiritual unity that was assisted by our denominational boundary.

The reason people think the church is divided today is that they think Christian unity is to be organizational. Martyn Lloyd-Jones wrote:

> A mere coalition of organisations or denominations has in reality nothing whatsoever to do with this unity. Indeed,

it may even be a danger. The unity that our Lord is concerned about is a unity which is spiritual. It consists of a unity of spirits, and it is a unity, therefore, which is based solidly upon the truth.[4]

James Montgomery Boice emphasized the same thing, writing:

This unity . . . is not organizational, where everyone must be forced into the same denomination. The worst times in the history of the church have been when everyone has been part of one large organization. It is not that kind of unity. The unity for which Jesus prayed is a unity patterned on the unity of the Father and the Son. That is, it is a unity of mind, will, love, and purpose.[5]

By this standard, the biblical ideal of Christian unity, we not only *can be* united, but if we are in Christ we *are* united. His Spirit lives in all true believers and unites us in truth, love, and purpose.

Discerning the Boundaries of Christian Unity

According to Paul, then, we do not create Christian unity but rather are to serve and promote the unity that already exists. When it comes to this, there are two main approaches. One is to say that since doctrine divides us, we must only insist on those doctrines upon which we all can agree. Doctrinal precision, much less doctrinal argument, is injurious to the church. This is undoubtedly the preferred model today, even among evangelicals; we must, we are told, have as minimal a creed as possible to serve the cause of unity. Paul's teaching in Ephesians, however, rules out this approach. He says there is "one Lord, one faith, one baptism" (Eph. 4:5). R. C. Sproul has observed: "The culture would like to say, 'One Lord, many faiths, many baptisms.'" But Paul insists that the one church has one faith and but one salvation, not many. Sproul explains why we must cultivate unity within the truth, rather than apart from truth:

> Yes, truth divides: it divides the sheep from the goats; it divides the gospel from heresy; it divides the Christ from the antichrist . . . Our culture preaches the doctrine of justification by a contentless faith. That is not Christianity; that is not biblical faith.[6]

The true church is not divided, Paul insists, for there is one church, one body. We have unity, but are now called to maintain and serve it, "eager to maintain the unity of the Spirit in the bond of peace" (Eph. 4:3). If we are to do this, we must rightly discern the boundaries of Christian unity and truth. If there is one church with one faith, then we must be prepared to discern what is the content that defines the boundary between brother Christians and false professors. With whom do we have unity? This is what we must discern.

In his outstanding book *Evangelicalism Divided,* Iain Murray tells the story of how this worked out among the English evangelicals in the 1960s. Martyn Lloyd-Jones, as we have already noted, held that the only real unity lay in the Spirit of God through faith in the gospel. But many evangelicals felt pressure from liberal members of the Anglican Church, who insisted that all baptized persons must be treated as Christians. Eventually, the evangelicals gave in to that pressure, agreeing that if you are baptized you are a Christian, even if you deny the deity of Christ and the atoning work of the cross.

This is of the greatest importance for us today, for this is the very principle being asserted among many evangelical and even Reformed writers. People speak of the "objectivity" of baptism in entering us into covenant with God. If this is the case, then baptism truly denotes the boundary of Christian unity.

But if we accept baptism as the boundary of Christian unity, then one does not need the gospel to be a Christian and the gospel is thereby relegated to the periphery, soon to be lost altogether. If baptism makes you a Christian, then we Protestants have a lot of apologizing to do for the Reformation, since it was in denial of this assertion that the Reformers turned the world upside down. If we admit to having Christian unity with anyone who is baptized, then we are on the high road back to Rome and the pope. Indeed, this is precisely the pattern being followed by the Church of England and by the liberal Lutheran denominations in their recent concords with Rome.

The English evangelicals found it difficult to tell baptized people who called themselves Christians that they could not be considered brothers and could not be partners in ministry. They were accused of divisiveness and a lack of love. We face the same difficulty today. But the alternative is to accept one church of many faiths, one Lord without his gospel. It was in rejecting this kind of unity that the English Reformers separated from Rome, many of them gladly accepting death rather than unity apart from the gospel.

Paul writes that there is "one Lord, one faith, one baptism" (Eph. 4:5). But does the Bible tell us where to draw the lines of this "one church, one faith"? Does Paul ever tell us where he drew the boundary between the church and unbelief? The answer is yes.

In 1 Corinthians he drew such a line: "Now I would remind you brothers, of the gospel I preached to you, which you received, in which you stand, and by which you are being saved, if you hold fast to the word I preached to you—unless you believed in vain" (1 Cor. 15:1–2). Paul is saying, "Here is the boundary of true Christianity; you must hold fast here or you are lost." He defines that boundary: "For I delivered to you as of first importance what I also received: that Christ died for our sins in accordance with the Scriptures, that he was buried, that he was raised on the third day in accordance with the Scriptures, and that he appeared to Cephas, then to the twelve" (1 Cor. 15:3–5). This is the boundary of the one Christian faith, Paul asserts, the biblical teaching concerning the death and resurrection of Jesus Christ. We must believe not only facts but also the doctrine tied to these facts. Jesus died "for our sins," not merely as a moral example or as a statement of God's love for us. The doctrine of substitutionary atonement is essential to Christianity; without believing it you are not a Christian. He goes on in that chapter especially to emphasize the resurrection, which was under attack in Corinth. Those who deny the resurrection are not Christians, he says, and cannot be saved.

Another instructive example is the Book of Galatians. Here was a church that Paul himself had founded, many of whose members he may have baptized. Yet he says, "I am astonished that you are so quickly deserting him who called you in the grace of Christ and are turning to another gospel—not that there is another one . . ." (Gal. 1:6–7). Paul says that to desert the one gospel he preached is to desert Christ. What does he say of someone who preaches a contrary gospel? Does he say, "Well, we surely have to admit that he is a brother, despite his petty doctrinal differences"? No, he says, "Let him be accursed" (Gal. 1:9).

What was the doctrinal problem in Galatia? It is noteworthy that the Galatians accepted the deity of Christ. They believed that Jesus died and rose from the grave. The facts of Christ's ministry were not in dispute. The problem was the doctrine concerning those facts, their implication for salvation. We often hear today that "the gospel is not the doctrine of justification, but the gospel is the fact of Jesus' death and resurrection, the mere declaration that Jesus is Lord." Let us note that none of those facts were in dispute in Galatia; it was the doctrine of justification by faith alone that Paul wrote to safeguard, and he considered those who denied it to be outside the pale of Christ's church. Paul insisted on unity in the gospel alone. That may mean more than justification by faith alone, but it cannot mean less, and we therefore cannot admit as part of the one church those who deny the gospel.

This is not the most pleasant part of Christian ministry, and none of us should make this our prime emphasis. But it is our duty. I am reminded here of the much neglected Book of Jude in the New Testament. What Jude says in the opening of his letter is something many of us feel very keenly. "Beloved," he says, "although I was very eager to write to you about our common salvation, I found it necessary to write appealing to you to contend for the faith that was once for all delivered to the saints" (Jude 3). I would rather not argue or engage in polemics, he says, and I really wanted just to write you about the wonderful truths in which we glory. But I have a duty, he says. "I found it necessary to contend for the faith," and it is necessary for us today as well. Why? Jude explains, "For certain people have crept in unnoticed who long ago were designated for this condemnation, ungodly people, who pervert the grace of our God . . ." (Jude 4). There are heretics and denials of the gospel, he notes, and that means he can't just write nice devotional material, though he would prefer to, but must contend for the faith so that it will be preserved for the church.

Jesus taught that there will be wolves in sheep's clothing; Paul commanded the Ephesian elders, "Pay careful attention to yourselves and to all the flock, in which the Holy Spirit has made you overseers, to care for the church of God, which he obtained with his own blood" (Acts 20:28). Following the example of our Lord and his apostles, out of love for the church, and as the duty of those appointed as shepherds over the flock, we must discern and safeguard the gospel boundary of true Christian unity. We cannot otherwise follow Paul's instruction to "maintain the unity of the Spirit in the bond of peace" in the church of which there is only "one Lord, one faith, one baptism, one God and Father of all."

Maintaining Unity among True Christians

That is only one half of the equation, however. For having discerned the true boundaries of the unified

33

church, we must then practice unity among all who are within those boundaries. It is our duty, based on this passage, to seek and promote and protect a feeling of unity and brotherhood, of love and cooperation, among all who adhere to the apostolic gospel that bounds the true church. This is something Francis Schaeffer passionately argued:

> The real chasm must be between true Bible-believing Christians and others, not at a lesser point. The chasm is not between Lutherans and everybody else, or Baptists and everybody else, or Presbyterians and everybody else . . . The real chasm is between those who have bowed to the living God and His Son Jesus Christ—and thus also to the verbal, propositional communication of God's Word, the Scripture—and those who have not.[7]

How is this possible, many respond, when we don't agree on everything? The answer is to be found in the manner in which we hold our disagreements within the fold of the true gospel church. Though we are organized outwardly in denominations, we must oppose the party spirit of denominationalism. The great Puritan Jeremiah Burroughs, a champion of truth but also notably charitable toward true believers with whom he disagreed, wrote this:

> We should labor to find out what is truth, search for it as silver, and go according to what light we have; but yet so, though we might differ, to 'keep the unity of the Spirit in the bond of peace,' and join in all things that we can, and so walk so lovingly that it may appear that, if there are differences, it is merely that which conscience makes,

because we dare not deny what we are persuaded in our consciences is a truth.[8]

In that spirit, true Christians may work together with a great sense of unity and love and purpose, despite any number of differences. Let's take baptism. There are brothers who sincerely, intelligently, based upon a careful reading of Scripture, hold a view of baptism that I am persuaded is mistaken. So long as we agree on the content and the centrality of the gospel, we have an evangelical unity despite our difference on baptism. Our unity is based on the gospel of the crucified and risen Lord Jesus Christ, received through faith alone by grace alone. The same can be said of other matters, such as end-times theories and church polity. Our unity is in Christ, in the gospel, and we are not surprised that we do not agree on everything or that we have different denominations. What we must avoid is the party spirit that makes the gospel secondary to other concerns.

If we know ourselves, and if we reflect on much of our past performance, we will realize the extent of the challenge here. How are we to attain and then maintain unity in the gospel? Paul tells us "to walk in a manner worthy of the calling to which [we] have been called, with all humility and gentleness, with patience, bearing with one another in love" (Eph. 4:1–2).

If we are to have unity within the true church, Paul says we must first be *humble*. Humility involves seeking the honor of others and being a servant. If we are to be humble, then in the matters in which we disagree, instead of belittling one another's views, instead of talking all the time, instead of trying to win the field, we must seek to understand and to profit from our brothers, to see the value of what they are saying. One of the principles we should uphold is sincerely seeking to understand the other position, charitably engaging it with our concerns. Furthermore, I do not mind saying that there are weaknesses and potential excesses in views I hold passionately—things like infant baptism, covenant theology, Presbyterian church government, and amillennialism. By humbly listening to the critiques of disagreeing brothers, I am protected against excessive tendencies among those who hold my positions, and the same happens when disagreeing brothers listen to my critiques.

Furthermore, Paul says, we must be *gentle* and *patient* with brothers and sisters in the one church of Jesus Christ. Gentleness means we do not seek to inflict wounds, nor to push opponents into the very positions we think injurious to their faith. This, in my mind, helps us in the Reformed faith to deal with people who hold the Arminian position. Can Arminians be true believers? That is a question you often hear. The answer is found by returning to the gospel: Do they hold to the apostolic teaching of the substitutionary atonement of Christ, his resurrection, and the gospel of justification by grace alone through faith alone? Most I have encountered do. I think they do so with vast inconsistencies and grave errors. But I think it a mistake to label theirs a different faith altogether. The same is true of some individual Roman Catholic believers who, despite the many errors they pick up from the official Vatican teaching, nonetheless have their hope firmly planted in the death and resurrection of Jesus Christ for forgiveness and new life. If they believe and trust the biblical gospel, then we must treat them with gentleness and patience as we seek to lead them into a more consistently biblical understanding of truth.

This is the value of rightly establishing the boundaries of the one faith. Outside of those boundaries we must treat such teachings as hostile. The apostles and our Lord never treated heretical teachings with gentleness, and they weren't very nice to heretical teachers either. But within the boundaries of gospel faith, we are dealing with people beloved of God and purchased by Christ with his blood. Even in our disagreements, we must treat these with gentleness and care.

Patience means that we are relying on the Holy Spirit's work. Most of us will admit that our theological understanding has grown over many years and often with real struggle. This is how it is for everybody, at least those who come to the Reformed faith. Knowing that spiritual struggle is involved in replacing unbelieving humanism with biblical truth, we don't have to win debates with true brothers and sisters; instead, we can communicate honestly, sincerely, biblically, and lovingly, while patiently and prayerfully leaving their persuasion in the Holy Spirit's hands.

Finally, Paul says to *bear with one another in love*. If we cannot do this, then we are missing out on the joy of being Christians. I don't have to agree with a true believer on everything to love him, to pray for her, or to worship together in holy communion. Indeed, if we cannot love each other while we are in disagreement over nonessentials, while we are still sinners who are liable to think and say and do foolish things, then we will not be able to enjoy the blessings of salvation until we get to heaven. What a failure that would be, and what a disgrace to the gospel and to our Lord who purchased us into his one body and commanded us to love.

I mentioned the little Book of Jude, where the apostolic leader so fervently opposes false teaching. But he concludes with words very much in line with Paul's words when it comes to genuine believers: "Have mercy on those who doubt; save others by snatching them out of the fire; to others show mercy with fear, hating even the garment stained by the flesh" (Jude 22–23).

Surely, it will take our whole lives to learn really how to do that. We often think how terrible it is that Christ does not give us full agreement in all things in this life so that we would be able to experience the fullness of love within the body. But perhaps we have it backward. On the one hand, we must develop these attributes Paul speaks of here—humility, gentleness, patience, long-suffering—in order to enjoy our unity. That is true. But perhaps the converse is truer. Perhaps the Lord leaves us with differences to work out in order to teach us how to love.

Isn't that the real work of our lives, to learn how to love other people? So God leaves intelligent brothers blind to what I think is the overwhelming evidence in favor of infant baptism, just so I can learn to be humble and gentle in relationship with them. God leaves me with whatever lack of understanding I have, just so my brothers can learn how to be patient and forbearing with a thickheaded person like me. The church is already one—we do not have to create church unity—but she has yet to come to maturity in the matter of love, which is our Lord's great command to his disciples. "Just as I have loved you," Jesus commanded, "you also are to love one another" (John 13:34). Jesus loved us while we were foolish sinners, and if we are to learn his love, it will have to be for one another in our foolishness and error and sin.

Worthy of the Gospel

I have made several references to the Church of England, not because I have a particular quarrel with that denomination, but because its history is so instructive. That is true not merely of its recent history, with its ecumenically minded archbishops, but even more so regarding its beginning.

I mentioned the origin of the Anglican Church in the preceding chapter, born of Henry VIII's desire for a son (thus his divorce), followed by the heavy-handed reforms during Edward VI's brief reign, and leading to the crucible years of Bloody Mary's fiery persecution. I pointed out the failure of the Protestant lords and religious leaders in their attempt to impose biblical religion upon the nation by force. In their praise, we should note that they rightly discerned the biblical boundaries for the one true Christian faith. These were the men who wrote the Thirty-Nine Articles and the Book of Common Prayer. They knew that there was only one church with only one faith, namely, that of the New Testament gospel. But during their six years of power in Edward's short reign, they showed little of the Christian spirit Paul considers to be worthy of the gospel: humility, gentleness, patience, and forbearance in love. They wanted one Lord, one faith, one baptism. But the brutality with which they sought it, and the personal riches and power the lords pursued along the way, made even true Christianity unpalatable to the spiritual mouths of their sheep.

There was a brief episode between the death of young King Edward and the ascension of Bloody Mary that illuminates our topic well. When it became clear, in 1553, that Edward was so sick he soon would die, the Protestant leaders hatched a plan to retain the throne. Though Mary was acknowledged by all as next in line, they coerced the dying Edward into abrogating the proper line of succession. In Mary's place, they put on the throne 16-year-old Lady Jane Grey, a cousin of Mary's and a fervent Protestant, though she was fourth in the true line of succession. Placing the crown on Jane's head and their hands on her shoulders, the lords and bishops thought they had made the Reformation safe in England.

Providence, however, did not cooperate. Attempts to arrest Princess Mary failed, and as the Protestant lords met in the Star Chamber, she began moving toward London. Everywhere she was hailed as queen. A popular uprising gained steam around a woman who was herself anything but popular. By the time Mary arrived in London, her claims were universally supported. Nine days into her rule, Lady Jane Grey had the crown toppled from her head and fell to her knees begging her elder cousin's forgiveness.

In the previous chapter I recalled the heroic martyrdoms of men like Latimer and Ridley, by which biblical religion was engraved on the heart of England. But I think it fair to say that this triumph of faith began in a small cell in the Tower of London, where Lady Jane Grey awaited her execution.

Lady Jane Grey is a fascinating figure of history and also a great Christian. She read the Greek Bible fluently, exchanged theological letters with Contintental Reformers like Bullinger, and agreed to accept the crown only out of obedience to her father and devotion to Christ. She was the kind of woman the church so greatly needs today—she is one of my heroes. Archbishop Carey no doubt would include Lady Jane among those who were guilty of dividing the church. She was a Christian unwilling to make the accommodations and compromises needed to oil the door of ecumenical partnership with Rome.

Lady Jane had been used, then abandoned by the Protestant lords, many of whom reverted to Catholicism to save their necks. Now she sat in a dark, damp cell, awaiting Bloody Mary's wrath. Wanting to make a trophy of her, and perhaps with a genuine concern for her soul, Mary sent her priest confessor, Feckenham, to secure Lady Jane's spiritual capitulation, to force her to profess one Lord by a different faith, namely the Roman Catholic faith. When the priest entered, Lady Jane knew that her life hung in the balance.

The famous interview was recorded word for word. First, Feckenham tried to get her to deny salvation by faith alone, arguing the Catholic position that works are necessary to be saved. Lady Jane replied, "I deny that, and I affirm that faith only saveth . . . we may not say that [works] profit to our salvation; for when we have done all, we are unprofitable servants, and faith only in Christ's blood saves us."

Next, he tried to make her profess transubstantiation, the doctrine that says we eat the physical body of Christ in the sacrament. The priest pointed out Jesus' statement, "Take, eat, this is my body." Jane replied, "I grant he saith so; and so he saith, I am the vine, I am the door; but he is never the more for that a door or a vine . . . God forbid that I should say that I eat the very natural body and blood of Christ; for then either I should pluck away my redemption, or else there were two bodies or two Christs, or twelve bodies, when his disciples did eat his body, and it suffered not till the next day."

Feckenham insisted that she must accept the pope's interpretation, but she responded, "No, I ground my faith upon God's word, and not upon the church; for if the church be a good church, the faith of the church must be tried by God's word, and not God's word by the church . . . And I say, that it is an evil church, and not the spouse of Christ, but the spouse of the devil, that alters the Lord's supper . . . Shall I believe this church? God forbid!"

Here was a courageous Christian who knew her Bible and was determined to serve one Lord by means of one faith only, namely that revealed by God in the Bible, even at the cost of her life. If she, and those great Christians who after her execution went to the stake for the gospel, had agreed that unity was more important than truth, then the English-speaking world might not even have the gospel today. Yet, with that said, it was not merely her holding of the truth, but Lady Jane's manner of holding the truth, not only with fellow believers but with adversaries who sought to take her life, that was so important. Her whole demeanor was cloaked in the majesty of Jesus

Christ, the nobility of the Holy Spirit, marked by humility, gentleness, patience, and forbearance.

This comes out especially at the interview's end. Disappointed, Feckenham took his leave, saying he was sorry for since she would not recant her doctrine, he was sure they would never meet again. The teenage princess replied with tears, "True it is that we shall never meet again, except God turn your heart; for I am assured, unless you repent, and turn to God, you are in an evil case; and I pray God, in the bowels of his mercy, to send you his Holy Spirit . . . to open the eyes of your heart."[9]

There is only one church, one faith, and one salvation. But there is also one manner in which they are worthily adorned in our lives: "with all humility and gentleness, with patience, bearing with one another in love." And since there is one church, both militant on earth and triumphant in heaven, then we are now one with Lady Jane Grey, and with Hugh Latimer and Nicholas Ridley and that whole generation of English martyrs, and with all the host of Christians in all lands throughout all generations who, bearing their crosses, followed the example of our Lord. Peter writes, "He committed no sin, neither was deceit found in his mouth. When he was reviled, he did not revile in return; when he suffered, he did not threaten, but continued entrusting himself to him who judges justly" (1 Peter 2:22–23). They are all one with us and we with them in Christ; Lady Jane and all the others are a great cloud of witnesses cheering us on, having left us an example not only of truth but also of love.

There is but one church, with one faith, and if we want to commend it to our generation to the glory of our

Lord, then we must walk, like those before us, in a manner worthy of Christ and of the calling to which we have been called.

> Though I may speak with bravest fire,
> and have the gift to all inspire,
> and have not love, my words are vain,
> as sounding brass, and hopeless gain.[10]

3

A HOLY CHURCH

1 CORINTHIANS 6:9–11

PHILIP G. RYKEN

---

*Do you not know that the unrighteous will not inherit
the kingdom of God? Do not be deceived: neither the
sexually immoral, nor idolaters, nor adulterers, nor
men who practice homosexuality, nor thieves, nor the
greedy, nor drunkards, nor revilers, nor swindlers will
inherit the kingdom of God. And such were some of
you. But you were washed, you were sanctified, you
were justified in the name of the Lord Jesus Christ and
by the Spirit of our God. —1 Corinthians 6:9–11*

---

*A*s we have noted in the preface, this book is based
on a series of addresses first delivered at the
2003 Philadelphia Conference on Reformation
Theology. I was present when we chose the church as our
theme. Inwardly, I groaned. *The church? Do we have to?*
Then we needed a title, and someone said, "What about
calling it 'One, Holy, Catholic, and Apostolic Church'?"

I wasn't very enthusiastic about that idea either. I said, "Can't we at least put 'Jesus' in there somewhere? I know I get a lot more excited about the church when I know he's involved." That is how we came up with the theme and title for the conference, "Christ and His Church."

My unenthusiastic response exposes my ambivalence about the church. Perhaps you are sometimes tempted to feel the same way. On the one hand, I love the church. One of my earliest memories is lying across my parents' laps as they sat in the front pews of Bethel Orthodox Presbyterian Church in Wheaton, Illinois. I also remember the minister standing up front, talking with his big black book. I had little or no idea what he was saying, but whatever it was, it was important, because everyone was listening to him.

Then all the other memories come flooding back: Making towers out of blocks in the nursery. Eating little pieces of bread and fish at Vacation Bible School. Hiding in the boiler room before the Junior Boys' Sunday school class. Reciting the catechism to Mrs. Brinks on Sunday evenings. Smelling the lilies on Easter Sunday. Sitting around the Harvey's living room studying the Bible and sharing prayer requests. Waiting nervously outside the pastor's study to meet with the elders and profess my faith in Jesus Christ. And most of all I remember going to worship week after week for my whole life, from when I was a little baby right up until last Sunday. Nothing has had a greater impact on my life than being in the church.

For me it has been like a friendship that eventually turns into a romance. Some couples fall in love first, and then get to know one another, but others start with friendship and the love comes later. This is the way it has been for me with the church. My relationship with the church started out as an ordinary part of life, and then one day I discovered that I was in love. I loved the public worship of God. I loved the preaching of his Word. I loved the administration of the sacraments. I loved the fellowship. It was love, true love.

Yet sooner or later anyone who loves the church becomes a wounded lover, because the sins of the church have a way of scarring our affections. People let us down. There is backbiting, gossip, and scandal. Church members have trouble getting along. Elders lord it over others. Ministers commit adultery. Congregations get divided. Denominations go into spiritual decline. And nothing is more heartbreaking than watching good churches go bad. Nothing is more painful than feeling betrayed by a brother or sister in Christ. Nothing is uglier than sin in the ministry. But these things happen, and sooner or later, anyone who tries to love the church suffers disappointment, disillusionment, and discouragement. Which is why I sometimes feel ambivalent about the church. I love the church, but it's not always easy to love.

Taking It by Faith

According to the Nicene Creed, we believe in "one *holy* church." The word "believe" is significant. The church's *unholiness* is something we have seen for ourselves, and thus we know it by sight. But the holiness of the church? This is something we can only believe by faith.

We believe that the church is holy because the Bible tells us so. Holiness is a prominent theme in the New Testament teaching about the church. What is the church? It is the holy people of God. We have "a holy calling" (2 Tim. 1:9); we are "set apart as holy" (2 Tim. 2:21); we were chosen to "be holy" (Eph. 1:4); we are "God's chosen ones, holy and beloved" (Col. 3:12). The Bible identifies us as "a holy priesthood" (1 Peter 2:5), "a holy nation" (1 Peter 2:9), and a holy temple (1 Cor. 3:17; cf. Eph. 2:21). In fact, this is why Jesus died on the cross. It was "so that he might present the church to himself in splendor, without spot or wrinkle or any such thing, that she might be holy . . ." (Eph. 5:27; cf. Col. 1:22).

The holiness of the church is the logic behind the remarkable word that the Bible uses to describe Christians: "saints"—literally, "the holy ones." The New Testament repeatedly uses this word to identify believers in Jesus Christ: "To the saints who are in Ephesus" (Eph. 1:1); "To all the saints in Christ Jesus who are at Philippi" (Phil. 1:1); "To the saints . . . in Christ at Colossae" (Col. 1:2). "Saint" is not a term the Bible reserves for a special category of Christians. Sainthood is not a lifetime achievement award—a merit badge for people who volunteer to teach junior high Sunday school, do door-to-door evangelism, and attend evening church. It is the term the Bible uses for every believer. The church is so holy that every one of its members is a saint.

At the same time, however, the Bible is brutally honest about the *un*holiness of the church. Nearly every epistle deals in one way or another with the painful reality of sin in the church. The apostles were forever pleading with people to turn away from sin and lead holy lives. Thus the New Testament is full of examples of false teaching, selfish ambition, sexual immorality, and discord.

Nevertheless, this is the church that God calls holy. What is true for individual Christians is also true for the church: *simul justus et peccator,* which means "at the same time righteous and a sinner." This was one of the key insights of the Reformation doctrine of justification by faith. As far as our own merits are concerned, we cannot be considered anything except sinners. But when we put our trust in Jesus Christ, God credits or imputes the righteousness of Jesus Christ to our account. On the basis of what Jesus has done, he reckons us as righteous, even before we are made perfect in holiness. John Calvin said that God "does not acquit us on a proof of our own innocence, but by an imputation of righteousness, so that though not righteous in ourselves, we are deemed righteous in Christ."[1]

This is true for Christians, and it is also true for the church. People generally want to put the righteous people and the sinners into two different categories, and usually we put ourselves with the righteous people. Other people may be sinners, but not us! There are many examples of this in church history: churches deciding to get rid of people who aren't holy (I am not referring here to the proper exercise of church discipline for scandalous and unrepentant sin, but to churches that are confident of their own righteousness). Usually such churches get smaller and smaller. Sometimes they disappear altogether. I know of two Reformed theologians who had such a narrow view of the church's purity that in the end they worshiped at home with their wives. In their humble opinion, no one else was holy enough to belong to their church (although one wonders whether their wives thought they were as holy as all that!).

It is all very well to say that the church is only for people who are holy, but what do we do when we find out that we are sinners too? Do we despair of ever becoming righteous and decide to leave the church? Do we lower the standard for righteousness far enough that we can still qualify? But of course this will not work either, because God refuses to lower his standards. His righteousness is his righteousness, and anyone who fails to measure up is a sinner.

What we need to understand is that, in spite of our sin, we are counted righteous in Christ. *Simul justus et peccator:* at the same time righteous and a sinner. This explains how a church entirely made up of sinners can still be defined as a holy church. With the exception of the prison system, the church is the only institution for bad people. It is for sinners in desperate need of God's grace. So here is a great mystery: it is as sinners that we belong to the holy church of Christ.

The Way We Were

One of the best places to see how these truths fit together is 1 Corinthians. The wickedness of Corinth was well known in the ancient world. Even among the pagans, the Corinthians had earned a reputation for all kinds of immorality, sexual and otherwise. Corinth was a difficult place to be the church.

Yet when Paul addressed the Christians in that city, he singled them out for their holiness: "To the church of God that is in Corinth, to those sanctified in Christ Jesus, called to be saints" (1 Cor. 1:2). The Corinthians were holy. They were sanctified saints. At the same time, however, Paul was fully aware that they were sinners. In the rest of the letter he deals with the most difficult forms of sin that any Christian leader can face: pride, quarreling, hard-heartedness, sexual immorality, discrimination, divorce, out-and-out idolatry—even acrimonious disputes about what kind of worship is pleasing to God.

This is the context for what Paul says about the church's holiness:

> Do you not know that the unrighteous will not inherit the kingdom of God? Do not be deceived: neither the sexually immoral, nor idolaters, nor adulterers, nor men who practice homosexuality, nor thieves, nor the greedy, nor drunkards, nor revilers, nor swindlers will inherit the kingdom of God. And such were some of you (1 Cor. 6:9–11).

Here Paul lists the prevailing vices of Corinthian culture. They also happen to be sins that are very common in America: sexual immorality, gluttony, greed, and corporate crime. He is not simply talking about people who are tempted by these sins, commit them against their better judgment, and repent with sadness and dismay. Rather, he is referring to people who give themselves over to these sins without remorse, whose lives are dominated by them. And he says that such people will not gain eternal life; they will be lost forever. The apostle needs to say this because of the way some of the Corinthians are living. They profess to be Christians, and they are going to church, but they are still leading pagan lives. Paul tells them that this is a fatal mistake. "Don't be deceived," he says. "The unrighteous will not inherit God's kingdom."

51

We need to take this warning seriously, because we live at a time when many people *are* deceived. The sins Paul mentions are exactly the kinds of sins that our culture promotes. During the 2003 War with Iraq, one Iraqi was asked why he was so happy that the Americans were coming. "Money, whiskey, sexy," he said. The reporters thought this was funny, but I doubt whether the apostle Paul would have seen the humor in it. He knew where these sins lead. Yet most people in our culture think there is absolutely nothing wrong with them. As far as they're concerned, greed is good, homosexuality is another lifestyle choice, and it's always time to party.

People in our culture are deceived. To them, Paul's list of soul-damning vices includes exactly the kinds of things they like to do! Isn't morality supposed to keep up with the times? Aren't we past all those old taboos? As one man said, after the head librarian at the University of Pennsylvania was exposed for using pornography, "Excuse me for being so naïve, but what's wrong with that?" This all-too-common attitude shows that we are living in a Corinthian culture, and thus we need to heed Paul's warning: "Don't be deceived." No matter what people say, these activities are as sinful as ever—so sinful that they lead straight to hell.

We like to pretend that sin—especially our own sin—isn't all that serious. We make excuses for ourselves, downplaying our depravity. But if we continue to indulge in unrepentant sin, we cannot inherit the kingdom of God. Our lives show that we have never come under the lordship of Jesus Christ. So we need to hear the apostle's message in our own times: "Look, if you give yourself over to sexual sin, or embrace the homosexual lifestyle, or drink your life away, or try to get more money any way you can, you will never get to heaven. That's obvious. It's common knowledge. So don't kid yourself. God is calling you to lead a holy life."

By listing these sins, Paul was not accusing the Corinthians of unrepentant immorality. He knew that most of them had left their old lifestyles behind. So he went on to say, "And such were some of you." This does not mean that the Corinthians never committed another sin, that they had reached some kind of sinless perfection or absolute sanctification. On the contrary, they continued to struggle with sin. This is evident from the kinds of issues Paul addresses in his letter. He tells the Corinthians how to deal with division in the church, honor God with their bodies, settle disputes, flee from idolatry, and stop hurting one another. They were still wrestling with the remnants of their old sinful nature.

What these verses *do* mean is that the Corinthians had made a definitive break with the dominating power of sin over their lives. A radical work of holiness had taken place. They were no longer living in unrepentant self-indulgence. They were no longer controlled by money, sex, and power. They were no longer defined by their depravity. Now they had a new identity in Christ and they had begun to live for God.

Holiness by Grace

What brought about this change? Or to ask the same question in a different way, what does it take for a church to be holy?

What it takes is nothing less than a supernatural work of divine grace. After describing their old sinful lifestyles, Paul writes, "And such were some of you. But you were washed, you were sanctified, you were justified in the name of the Lord Jesus Christ and by the Spirit of our God" (1 Cor. 6:11). There are three main verbs in this verse: washed (*apelousasthe*), sanctified (*hēgiasthēte*), and justified (*edikaiōthēte*).

These verbs have several things in common. They all occur in the past tense. Also, they all refer to things that happened at some point in the past: the Corinthians were washed, sanctified, and justified. Another feature these verbs share is that they are all passives (technically, *apelousasthe* is a middle, but here it has the force of a passive). In other words, they do not tell what the Corinthians did, but what they had done *to* them. It is like the all-important difference between "I hit you with my car" and "I was hit by your car." What the police officer wants to know is who hit whom! Paul is clear in this passage as to who did the washing, the sanctifying, and the justifying. These were not things the Corinthians did for themselves, but things that were done for them by God the Holy Spirit. Salvation is not something we accomplish on our own. Rather, our holiness comes by grace.

All three verbs go together. This is true grammatically. In Greek the word "but" occurs before each verb. To be technical, we could translate the verse like this: "But you were washed, *but* you were sanctified, *but* you were justified." This may not be the way we write good English, but it shows that these terms are connected. Rather than outlining three separate steps in the plan of salvation—first, we get washed, then we get sanctified, and finally we get justified—these words describe the total change that takes place when we come to faith in Christ. Whether we describe this change as being washed, sanctified, or justified, the point is that in Christ we have a whole new holy life.

You were washed. First comes the word "washed," which is a strong word for cleansing. It means to wash away something filthy until it is totally clean. The sins the Corinthians had committed made them filthy right down to their very souls. But they were washed.

Many people assume that this refers explicitly to baptism. This would make good sense. Baptism is the sacrament that marks our entrance into the covenant community of the church, and thus it would be appropriate to put it first in a list of things that divide the old life of sin from the new life of holiness. Furthermore, the physical sign in baptism is washing with water. Thus it is easy to understand why this verse is sometimes taken as a reference to baptism.

The trouble is that the word used here is not the biblical term for baptism; it is a more general term for washing. If Paul had wanted to say that the Corinthians were baptized, he could have and he probably would have, but he didn't. Instead, he said that they were *washed.* By doing this, he was pointing to the spiritual reality of cleansing from sin by the Holy Spirit's regenerating work, based on the atoning blood of Christ. To be washed in this sense means to be morally and spiritually purified. It is the kind of washing David had in mind when he wrote: "wash me, and I shall be whiter than snow" (Ps. 51:7). To be washed is to be cleansed from the filth of sin.

We can still make a connection here with baptism, because baptism signifies cleansing from sin—the same kind of cleansing Paul is referring to here. It is not water baptism itself that makes us clean. What makes us clean is the atoning blood of Jesus Christ (1 John 1:7). But the sacrament of baptism is a physical sign pointing to the spiritual reality of cleansing from sin. So although 1 Corinthians 6:11 is not about baptism, exactly, we can say that baptism is about the same thing that the verse is about: purification. Washing is an inward reality to which the outward sign of baptism also points.

So when were the Corinthians washed? Probably at conversion, when the Holy Spirit took the saving work of Jesus Christ and made it theirs by granting them the gift of faith. Elsewhere Paul calls this "the washing of regeneration" (Titus 3:5). It is the spiritual transformation that takes place when the Holy Spirit washes a sinner clean.

You were sanctified. The second verb Paul uses is "sanctified." What makes this confusing is that here sanctification comes before justification, whereas elsewhere in the New Testament justification comes first. It is also confusing because here sanctification is put in the past tense (see also 1 Cor. 1:2), but in most other places it is described as an ongoing process. What is Paul saying?

It helps to remember the original meaning of sanctification. To be sanctified is to be set apart for holiness. We see this in the Old Testament, where God taught his people what it meant to be holy by setting certain things apart from their common use and dedicating them for his service. The tabernacle was set apart from the rest of the camp as sacred space for the worship of God. Within the tabernacle, the holy of holies was set apart as the place where the high priest went to make atonement. The Sabbath was set apart from the other days of the week as sacred time for holy rest. The priests were set apart from the people as the holy servants of God. Certain foods were set apart from other foods. God was always making a distinction, setting things apart for his service.

By doing this, God was setting himself apart as the holy God. God is so infinitely pure in his divine being that he has to be separated from sinners. The Israelites were reminded of this by everything from the way their camp was set up to what they were allowed to eat. God was constantly reminding them of his holiness, and at the same time showing what it meant for them to be holy. In the Old Testament regulations he was saying, "Be holy, for I am holy" (Lev. 11:44; cf. Matt. 5:48; 1 John 3:3). The Israelites were set apart as God's holy people. They were separated from the world in order to be consecrated to God. As God said, "My holy name I will make known in the midst of my people Israel . . . And the nations shall know that I am the LORD, the Holy One in Israel" (Ezek. 39:7). This is what it means to be sanctified; it means to be set apart for God.

With this background in mind, we are in a position to apply the same principle to the Christian life. When were we set apart for God? Usually, when we think about the doctrine of sanctification, we think of the ongoing process by which the Holy Spirit conforms us to the image of Christ, making us more and more godly. This is a process—a long process—that will not end until we get to glory. It is not something we would ever describe in the past tense because there is so much more work that still needs to take place. The Bible calls this process of transformation "sanctification."

However, we were also sanctified when we first came to Christ. We were sanctified in the sense that we were set apart for holiness. In his excellent book on the church, Edmund Clowney rightly states that the Bible "does not restrict the language of holiness to God's ongoing work . . . When God makes us his own through the work of the Spirit in our hearts, he sets us apart, claiming us as his holy children."[2] This does not mean that we become perfectly holy all at once. There are still sins we need to confess and areas of obedience in which we need to grow. Sanctification is a lifelong process. But what it does mean is that we were set apart for God from the moment we first believed. We have made a definitive break with all the sins that used to motivate us and dominate us. In a word, we were sanctified.

To give an analogy, it is like the aftermath of the War with Iraq. The old regime of Saddam Hussein ended several weeks into the war, and in one sense the country was liberated. The moment of liberation came when Saddam Hussein's statue was toppled in the heart of Baghdad; at that moment, the nation was separated from the old regime. Nonetheless, the war was not yet over and the hard work of nation building had only just begun.

Something similar happens in the life of a believer. There was a decisive moment when we gave our lives to Jesus Christ, and in that moment the old regime of sin came to an end. We could even say that in that moment we were sanctified. On the basis of Christ's saving work on the cross, the Holy Spirit set us apart as belonging to

God. He also gave us a seed of holiness that will grow and spread throughout our lives. So both of these things are true: we *were* sanctified, and we *are being* sanctified. But what Paul wanted the Corinthians to understand was the former: they were sanctified.

You were justified. The third word Paul used to describe the church's holiness, "justified," came from a court of law. Not only were the Corinthians cleansed by the washing of the Holy Spirit, and not only were they set apart by his sanctifying grace, but they were also justified in the name of Jesus Christ.

To justify is to render a favorable verdict. It is to declare that, from the law's standpoint, a person is in the right. He is not guilty, but innocent. Donald Grey Barnhouse used to illustrate this by telling the story of Bertram Campbell, a man who spent three years and four months in Sing Sing prison for a forgery he didn't commit. When the real criminal finally confessed, Campbell was taken before the governor of New York to receive a pardon. Except in this case a pardon really wasn't appropriate, because the language of a pardon assumed that the man was guilty. So in Campbell's case the governor changed the traditional wording from "fit object of our mercy" to "innocent of the crime for which he was convicted."[3] He was not simply pardoned; he was justified.

In the Bible justification has to do with our legal standing before God. It is God's declaration that we are righteous at the bar of his justice. On the face of things, this would seem to be the wrong verdict for God to reach about the Corinthians, because they were not righteous. Quite the opposite. First Corinthians 6:9–10 lists some of the things they had done and identifies them as the deeds of unrighteous people. Nevertheless, the Corinthians were justified; they were legally declared righteous. How can this be? How can God justify the ungodly, as the Bible says he does?

The answer comes at the end of verse 11: the Corinthians were justified in the name of Jesus. That is to say, they were declared righteous on the basis of what Jesus had done rather than on the basis of what they had done. This is the only way a sinner can ever be justified. We cannot be justified on our own merits, because we don't have any. We can only be justified by the perfect life, the atoning death, and the victorious resurrection of Jesus Christ. The Heidelberg Catechism asks, "How are you righteous before God?" The answer is:

> Only by true faith in Jesus Christ. In spite of the fact that my conscience accuses me that I have grievously sinned against all the commandments of God, and have not kept any one of them, and that I am still ever prone to all that is evil, nevertheless, God, without any merit of my own, out of pure grace, grants me the benefits of the perfect expiation of Christ, imputing to me his righteousness and holiness as if I had never committed a single sin or had ever been sinful, having fulfilled myself all the obedience which Christ has carried out for me, if only I accept such favor with a trusting heart (A. 60).

The Heidelberg Catechism answers in the singular, but we could give the same answer in the plural. How are *we* righteous before God? "Only by true faith in Jesus Christ. In spite of the fact that we have broken all the

60

commandments of God, nevertheless, out of his pure grace, God imputes to us the righteousness of Christ as we receive him by faith."

This is what it takes to make the church holy. And remember how remarkable it is that this is even possible. It's amazing: there is actually a way for the church—yes, the church, with all its sin!—to be holy. The only way it is possible is by the saving work of a sovereign God. We do not make ourselves holy. Remember, the verbs in 1 Corinthians 6:11 are (divine) passives. They explain what God has done for us rather than what we have done for God. The Christian life is not a program for self-improvement; it is a divine work of grace. We are not holy by any reason of our own spiritual accomplishment, but by the mercy of God in Christ. As the Scripture says, "You were washed, you were sanctified, you were justified in the name of the Lord Jesus Christ and by the Spirit of our God."

A Call to Holiness

Do you believe in the holiness of the church? This is something we believe, not so much because we have seen it, but because the Bible tells us that it is true.

At the beginning of this chapter I said that I get a lot more excited about the church when I know that Jesus is going to be part of it. This is exactly what we see in 1 Corinthians 6: God making us holy in Christ. The Holy Spirit takes what Jesus did in his death and resurrection and makes it ours through faith, washing us, sanctifying us, and justifying us. Thus the holiness of the church is a gospel holiness. It is based on the saving work of Jesus

Christ on the cross and through the empty tomb. In the words of Puritan theologian John Owen, "Holiness is nothing but the implanting, writing and realizing of the gospel in our souls."[4]

Sometimes I think about this on Sunday mornings as I look out at the congregation of Tenth Presbyterian Church in Philadelphia. I think about many things while I'm sitting up on the platform behind the pulpit. I try to make eye contact with my children. I see people that I know are in need and I pray for them. I notice who's sitting with whom, and whether they've started sharing a hymnal yet, so I know how serious their relationship is getting.

But sometimes I reflect on what God has done to make his people holy. As a church we are not holy in ourselves, and I probably know this better than anyone else. Nevertheless, we are holy to God in Christ. I think of the cleansing we have received in our regeneration, in which God washes away our sin. I think of the sanctification we have received in our calling, in which God sets us apart for his service. I think of the grace we have received in our justification, in which God counts us righteous through the cross of Christ. How could anyone be ambivalent about the church? Its sin notwithstanding, and in spite of all the people we find hard to love, the church is the holy people of God.

If we are holy, then we should lead holy lives. We should heed the practical exhortation that the apostle Paul gave in his next letter to the Corinthians: "Let us cleanse ourselves from every defilement of body and spirit, bringing holiness to completion in the fear of God" (2 Cor. 7:1). Here is a significant phrase: "bringing holiness to completion." Paul reminded the Corinthians that they were holy to God. After all, they were washed, they were sanctified, and they were justified. Nevertheless, their holiness still needed to be brought to completion. God was calling them to become what they were in Christ, and this required the pursuit of holiness.

Sadly, this pursuit is uncommon in the contemporary church. More often people who claim to be Christians pursue the same selfish ambitions, worship the same worthless idols, enjoy the same sinful pleasures, watch the same ungodly entertainments, and grasp for the same greedy possessions as everyone else. There is shockingly little difference between the way that Christians and non-Christians behave. A recent report from the Princeton Religion Research Center claimed, "Religion Is Gaining Ground, but Morality Is Losing Ground." The report showed how increases in church attendance and Bible reading have been offset by a simultaneous decline in morality among churchgoers.[5] This is a strange combination: supposedly people are more religious, and yet at the same time their conduct is less moral. What this shows is the absence of real gospel holiness—a passion to do what is right before God.

As a result, the church is ineffective in its witness to the world. We lack the kind of personal and corporate holiness that would recommend the truth of the gospel to our culture. Instead, our message is compromised by our sin. One of the great weaknesses—maybe *the* great weakness—of the church today is the absence of radical godliness that would set us apart from the world. As Mark Dever often says, as Christians we need to be distinct from the world, and not simply lost in it. The holy church is to shape the culture, not to be shaped by it.

This is what Paul was urging the Corinthians to understand. Why did he remind them of everything that God had done to make them holy? Was it so they could relax? If they were already holy by grace, why bother to pursue practical godliness? But of course Paul wrote with exactly the opposite purpose in mind. Far from telling them to relax, he was urging them to greater holiness. He reminded them about what they were before they became Christians so that they would resist the temptation to return to their old ways of life, but instead would strive to become the people God wanted them to be in Christ. What motivates us to lead holy lives is not the desperate thought that we need to make ourselves good enough for God, but a profound gratitude for what God has done for us in Christ.

Here are some questions for self-examination: Do I have a passion for holiness? Am I putting sin to death? Am I taking new steps of obedience? Am I asking God the Holy Spirit to help me grow in godliness? Am I resisting and rejecting the sins that Paul mentions in this chapter, the temptations to lust and greed? Have I made the resolution that Jonathan Edwards made when he was a young man, "Never to give over, nor in the least to slacken my fight with my corruption, however unsuccessful I may be"?[6]

If we are in the church, then God is calling us to a life of holiness, and 1 Corinthians is a good place to start. Here God calls us to be holy in the way we handle our disagreements, holy with respect to marriage and divorce, holy in our sexuality, holy in the way we handle our singleness, holy when we are tempted to bow down to the idols of this age, holy in our respect for the gifts of others, and holy in our worship. When we are confronted with the temptation to sin—as we are every day—we need to say, "I am holy for Christ, and I want to live in a way that is pleasing to him." This is the way God calls us to live because only this kind of life is in keeping with his character: "As he who called you is holy, you also be holy in all your conduct, since it is written, 'You shall be holy, for I am holy'" (1 Peter 1:15–16).

Future Holiness

In 1994 I attended the celebrations for the 350th anniversary of the Westminster Confession of Faith. At the close of those celebrations, the Scottish minister Eric Alexander asked a series of provocative questions: "What is the really important thing that is happening in the world in our generation? Where are the really significant events taking place? What is the most important thing? Where do you need to look in the modern world to see the most significant event from a divine perspective? Where is the focus of God's activity in history?" He answered by saying:

> The most significant thing happening in history is the calling, redeeming, and perfecting of the people of God. God is building the church of Jesus Christ. The rest of history is simply a stage God erects for that purpose. He is calling out a people. He is perfecting them. He is changing them. History's great climax comes when God brings down the curtain on this bankrupt world and the Lord Jesus Christ arrives in his infinite glory. The rest of history is simply the scaffolding for the real work.[7]

To illustrate his point, Alexander referred to the building where some of our meetings were held: London's Westminster Abbey. He remarked that the last time he had been at the Abbey, its stone was black and the whole front of the building was covered with scaffolding. But something was happening behind that scaffolding. People were busy cleaning the building, trying to bring out its true beauty. And when the scaffolding was finally taken down, the Abbey was revealed in gleaming, pristine white stone.

God is doing the same thing with the church. Alexander concluded by saying, "There will come a day when God will pull down the scaffolding of world history. Do you know what he will be pointing to when he says to the whole creation, 'There is my masterpiece?' He will be pointing to the church of Jesus Christ."[8]

This is what we mean when we say that we believe in one holy church. We are certainly not making any great claims about our own righteousness. Nor are we denying the corrupting influence that sin—including our own sin—still has on the church. But we are testifying that by the grace he has shown us in Jesus Christ—his washing, sanctifying, justifying grace—God has called us to be holy, and he will not stop until our holiness is perfected in glory.

4

A CATHOLIC CHURCH

GALATIANS 3:26–29

MARK E. DEVER

For in Christ Jesus you are all sons of God, through faith. For as many of you as were baptized into Christ have put on Christ. There is neither Jew nor Greek, there is neither slave nor free, there is neither male nor female, for you are all one in Christ Jesus. And if you are Christ's, then you are Abraham's offspring, heirs according to promise. —Galatians 3:26–29

*T*he Nicene Creed (completed in A.D. 381) defines the church's attributes as "one, holy, catholic, and apostolic." We now come to that third attribute—catholic. What does "catholic" mean?

Though few today remember it, considering a Catholic presidential candidate was an explosive issue in twentieth-century American politics. Not just in 1960, when Roman Catholic John F. Kennedy was elected president, but much more so in 1928. In that year, the Republican nominee, Herbert Hoover, faced the popular Democratic governor of New York, Al Smith. Smith was also the first Roman Catholic to be nominated by a major party for the office of President of the United States. Anti-Catholic rumors abounded. Protestant marriages were to be annulled. The pope was preparing to move to America. The new Holland Tunnel was being secretly extended to the Vatican.

To alleviate concerns, Governor Smith traveled to Oklahoma City in September to give a major speech on the matter of religion. His speech was quickly forgotten when, the following night, in the same auditorium, the pastor of Calvary Baptist Church of New York City, John Roach Straton, came and gave a speech entitled "Al Smith and the Forces of Hell," denouncing Smith's Catholicism. He equated Smith with the urban evils of "card playing, cocktail drinking, poodle dogs, divorces, novels, stuffy rooms, dancing, evolution, Clarence Darrow, overeating, nude art, prize-fighting, actors, greyhound racing, and modernism."[1]

One eastern lady who had come to Oklahoma to support Smith and speak for him had a run-in with a lady from a small town, who was a devout Baptist. "So you be the woman speaker, be you?" said the Oklahoman. "And you're for Smith?"

"Yes," said the eastern lady.

"Well, I ain't."

"Perhaps if you would let me talk to you, I might change your mind," said the Smith supporter.

"No you couldn't," said the old woman. "Smith's one of them Catholics and they brought in sprinklin'!"[2]

That episode not only highlights the challenge facing us with regard to the catholicity of the church, but also challenges the wisdom of having a Southern Baptist minister like me make a contribution to this book on the topic, "A Catholic Church"!

Introduction

What is the church's catholicity? Why is it significant for us to consider this from the perspective of Reformation theology?

Most of us become familiar with the term "catholic" by means of the Roman Catholic Church. In so naming itself, the Roman church claims that it alone is the truly catholic church. Its arguments are several: (1) Only Rome has a unified, world-wide authority; (2) only Roman Catholics exist in every country; (3) only they have always existed since Christ; (4) only they have the fullness of grace and truth; and (5) only they are the majority of those who call themselves Christians. In short, they claim to be everywhere and always. As their motto puts it, they are *semper eadem,* always the same.

I cannot affirm that "catholic" is an accurate description of that visible organization which is in submission to the authority of the bishop of Rome, the pope. In fact, the two words Roman and Catholic together—one limiting, and the other universal—make up an oxymoron. No one church alone can rightly be called *the* catholic church.

The word "catholic" comes from the Greek word *katholikos,* which means "whole, entire, complete, general, universal." While this adjective is nowhere used of the church in the New Testament, or of anything else, the

69

adverbial form of it does appear once in Acts, where the apostles are commanded not to speak or preach *at all* (*katholou*) in the name of Jesus (Acts 4:18). The simple equivalent for "catholic" in modern English is the adjective "universal." Such universality is not the attribute of any one group of true Christians alone.

"Universal" or "catholic" is used primarily in opposition to "local." While a local church is indigenous in the sense that its members are taken from the local population and it is able to congregate all together, its nature is heavenly. That heavenly nature is in Christ, and therefore can participate in the same unity, holiness, and apostolicity that all other truly Christian churches participate in, regardless of where they may be located. In one sense, *the catholicism of the church is simply its other attributes—unity, holiness, apostolicity—appearing everywhere and anytime there has been a true church or true Christians.*

So the church's catholicity is the simple acknowledgement that the church is not confined to any one place or people. In that sense it is not like the Jewish nation, which was limited to the bounds of one nation.

In this chapter, we will first examine catholicity historically and exegetically, and then consider some practical implications of the church's catholic nature.

"Catholic": A Historical Approach and Assessment

First, let us consider the use of the word "catholic"— and the idea behind it—historically. The first known use of this word in connection with the church was in Ignatius of Antioch's letter to the Smyrnaeans, written around

A.D. 112. Ignatius mentions that "where Jesus Christ is there is the universal church." Early writers believed in the catholic church in the sense that they believed that Christians everywhere trusted one God, confessed one faith, had one baptism, and shared one mission. In that sense, "catholic church" first meant real or authentic church.

From about the third century on, the word came to be used as particularly synonymous with orthodoxy. So, the "catholic" church was opposed to a heretical or schismatic church. Clement of Alexandria, around A.D. 200, wrote:

> The one Church is violently split up by the heretics into many sects. In essence, in idea, in origin, in pre-eminence we say that the ancient Catholic Church is the only church. This Church brings together, by the will of the one God through the one Lord . . . those who were already appointed; whom God fore-ordained, knowing before the world's foundation that they would be righteous.[3]

By the middle of the fourth century, in addition to the idea of authentic and orthodox (as opposed to false), the word had incorporated the idea of the church's extensive reach to every land and every class of person. Cyril of Jerusalem, lecturing to those preparing for baptism around A.D. 350, clearly had this idea of what the word "catholic" meant. He said that the church

> is called Catholic then because it extends over all the world, from one end of the earth to the other; and because it teaches universally and completely one and all the doctrines which ought to come to men's knowledge, concerning things both visible and invisible, heavenly and

earthly; and because it brings into subjection to godliness the whole race of mankind, governors and governed, learned and unlearned; and because it universally treats and heals the whole class of sins, which are committed by soul or body, and possesses in itself every form of virtue which is named, both in deeds and words, and in every kind of spiritual gifts.[4]

In A.D. 381 the Nicene Creed defined the attributes of the church as "one, holy, catholic and apostolic." By the middle of the next century, the word "catholic" was inserted in the Apostles' Creed. By the eleventh century, when the eastern and western churches divided, the eastern writers preferred the description "Orthodox," while those in the west used the description "Catholic," with both saying essentially the same thing. So from the second or third century until the modern period, the word "catholic" was a term used for exclusion and definition, to mark off regular from irregular, similar to the way modern conservative American Christians might say something is "evangelical" rather than a "cult."[5]

As regional heresies sprang up in the early church, the term "catholic" was important in the battle for truth. Powerful apologists like Augustine refuted the heretics or schismatics by asking them how they could claim to be the universal church when their teaching could not be found in most places where the church was. In the early fifth century, Vincent of Lerins, a monk, laid down a threefold test for what is truly catholic—what has been believed everywhere, always, and by all. This has been called the Vincentian Canon and has been used, particularly by the church of Rome, to evaluate the worth of various traditions.

As you can well understand, the Vincentian Canon proved to be difficult for the sixteenth-century Reformers. This was difficult because the Protestants were not everywhere (they were only in Europe) and they had not always existed. "Where was your church before Luther?" was the taunt. And the Protestants were not all the people of Christendom—their numbers were very small compared to those of the church of Rome.

In what sense, then, could the new Protestant churches claim to be "catholic"? Luther and Calvin gave primacy to the "always" in the definition of catholicity, not to the "everywhere" and "by all" aspects. They defined "universal" or "catholic" as a category not primarily about space but about time, not about the church's spatial extensiveness but about its temporal continuity. In this sense, they spoke of their continuity with the apostolic church.

The Heidelberg Catechism asks, "What believest thou concerning the 'Holy Catholic Church' of Christ?" It answers, "That the Son of God, from the beginning to the end of the world, gathers, defends and preserves to himself, by his Spirit and word, out of the whole human race, a church, chosen to everlasting life, agreeing in true faith; and that I am, and for ever shall remain, a living member thereof" (A. 54).

Ursinus commented:

> The Church is called *catholic, first* in respect to place; because it is spread over the whole world, and is not tied or restricted to any particular place, kingdom, or certain succession. The catholicity of the church, in this respect, commenced at the time of the Apostles; because prior to this time the church was circumscribed in narrow limits,

being confined to the Jewish nation. *Secondly,* in respect to men, because the church is gathered from all classes of men of every nation. *Thirdly,* in respect of time, because it will endure throughout every period of the world: "I will be with you always even to the end of the world"; and because there is only one true Church of all times, which is of such a peculiar constitution as to embrace the whole world, and not to be tied down to any one particular place.[6]

Since the church of Rome differed from the apostolic church's teaching, it could not claim such temporal universality.

Among Protestants this idea of temporal catholicity— that is, that the church existing now is the same church in which the apostles were and are—has replaced, or at least largely supplanted, thoughts of catholicity in terms of space alone. In that sense, catholicity among Protestants has seemed very much like apostolicity. To be apostolic is to be catholic, and to be catholic is to be apostolic, because the widespread acceptance of a teaching among self-confessed Christians is one of the marks of the truth of the teaching. The sense of the faithful is not unerring, but is normally correct.

What a comfort and encouragement this truth is to us! As James Bannerman put it:

> The assemblies of Christians in every quarter of the globe, who worship God in sincerity and truth, are one in such a sense as their distance from one another admits of; and they must all be regarded as branches of the universal Church of Christ throughout the world—the great community of believers, separated by distance and kindred and tongue, who cannot meet together in the body, but

who really meet together in the Spirit. The invisible Church of Christ on earth is local, but it is also catholic.[7]

Let me speak to Baptists particularly for a moment. Some Baptists have had a great reluctance to speak of any universal church at all, other than that final assembly of all the redeemed in heaven. Where does this hesitancy come from? This reluctance has been there not because we have thought that we are the only Christians. We do not think that now, nor have we ever believed it. But there are a few other reasons, each related to the others.

In part, this reluctance has come because of the understanding—common among Protestants—that the nearly universal definition of the church in the New Testament is "congregation." This was so much taken to be the case that William Tyndale (in his great work which stands behind all of our English translations of the Bible) simply translated *ekklēsia* as "congregation." This strand of "congregation-only" ecclesiology has survived in various corners of Protestantism, including the nineteenth-century Landmark movement among Baptists, a movement that still has strength in many congregations.

Another part of Baptist reluctance to understand the visible church as having a catholic aspect on earth is the underlying assumption of many Christians that a visible church must have a visible organization. In a strange way, the Baptist insistence on the primacy of the congregational understanding of the church has led to our own kind of ecumenism. We share with most other Christians the idea that Christ's church should be one, and we are confident that it is, and that this unity will one day be manifested perfectly. But before the Lord's return, we feel that no officers, no organization, no polity has been given to all of that portion of the universal church which happens to be militant (alive) and visible at any one time, except for the officers, organization, and polity of the local congregation. We may cooperate together with other Christians, but no organization of human invention (e.g., popes, general assemblies, or conventions) should be allowed to usurp the biblically mandated authority of the local congregation gathered.

Still a third source of reluctance among Baptists to speak easily of the universal church as encompassing all visible Christian churches has been our difficulty in understanding the existence of true (or at least regular) churches without the practice of baptism (which we understand to be only of believers). We would no sooner admit unbaptized persons to membership than would those of you who are our paedobaptist brothers and sisters; and we have reached different conclusions than you have about what baptism is. These three considerations—or some combination of them—have led some Baptists and other evangelicals to sometimes deny the reality of the universal church anywhere other than in heaven.

But, the hesitations of some evangelicals aside, the New Testament in Matthew 16:18, in Ephesians (1:22–23; 3:10, 21; 4:4; 5:23–32) and elsewhere (1 Cor. 10:32; 11:22; 12:28; Col. 1:18, 24; Heb. 12:23), clearly speaks of a church that is not merely local, but universal and catholic, and yet exists not only in the future, but now in this world. It needs no earthly head to create its unity; Christ alone is its head. It is marked by the Word rightly preached, and by baptism and the Lord's Supper rightly administered to believers (and, some would say, to their children). It is this church—the universal church—and no one local church that has inherited the church's universal mission that Christ set out in Matthew 28.

Sometimes we quote approvingly John Wesley's comment that "the world is my parish." And when we set Wesley's statement over against a narrow parochialism that appears unconcerned about what goes on outside one's own immediate community or sphere of responsibility, we can appreciate what he is saying. The sentiment is correct, even admirable.

However, strictly taken, Wesley's statement is false. Ride however many thousands of miles on horseback he might—being in Newcastle and Bristol every year—the world could never be Wesley's parish. He was limited in space and limited in time. His mission was limited. No single Methodist chapel was the universal church. Nor was the whole Methodist conference, nor the church of England, nor all the Protestant churches in the eighteenth century.

Having said all that, there is still a sense in which it is right that each Christian have a concern for all other Christians elsewhere, as God gives opportunity. After all, the universal church stretches across time from the cross to the consummation, and across space from Jerusalem to London to Buenos Aires to Tokyo. And these local churches are all our extended family in Christ. This is the reality of the catholic church.

"Catholic": Paul's Argument in Galatians

Although this "attribute" of the church is not talked about explicitly in Scripture, cherishing it helps us to cherish the gospel, because it is rooted in the very dispute that is at the center of the New Testament from Acts on—the question of whether the church would be Jewish or would be multinational and multiethnic. Paul, in Galatians, understood this question to be closely entwined with the very gospel itself. Let's turn now to the Book of Galatians and remind ourselves of what Paul was contending for there.

Could both Jews and Gentiles be children of Abraham, and of God's promises to Abraham? Basically, could they be children of God? Did it matter who their parents were or what nation they resided in? Though Paul didn't state the question in these words, you could also ask, "Is Christ's Church Catholic?" Here is Paul's answer:

> For in Christ Jesus you are all sons of God, through faith. For as many of you who were baptized into Christ have put on Christ. There is neither Jew nor Greek, there is neither slave nor free, there is neither male nor female, for you are all one in Christ Jesus. And if you are Christ's, then you are Abraham's offspring, heirs according to promise. (Gal. 3:26–29)

How are you forgiven of your sins, freed from its penalty and power, and adopted into God's family? The false teachers among the Galatians evidently thought they were saved through Christ, but they didn't accept the idea that salvation came through Christ alone. They may have even thought that they had accepted the idea of faith in Christ being the way these blessings come; but they had certainly not understood that it is by faith alone, and not by observing the law. It is in this way that the church's catholicity becomes directly important to Paul's teaching of the gospel.

Paul addresses the problem in Galatia in an earlier chapter, asking a series of questions:

> O foolish Galatians! Who has bewitched you? It was before your eyes that Jesus Christ was publicly portrayed as crucified. Let me ask you only this: Did you receive the Spirit by works of the law or by hearing with faith? Are you so foolish? Having begun by the Spirit, are you now being perfected by the flesh? Did you suffer so many things in vain—if indeed it was in vain? Does he who supplies the Spirit to you and works miracles among you do so by works of the law, or by hearing with faith? (Gal. 3:1–5)

If you asked these people how they had received the Spirit, how they had been justified before God and declared innocent before him, how they had been freed from the penalty of sin and were even now being saved from the power of sin, as God had included them in his family—if you asked these Christians how all of these wonderful things had happened, you would find that there was a confusion arising among them.

Some were saying that all of this happened because they observed the law. Others knew that all of this had happened simply because they had believed the gospel of Christ, which they had heard. Who can say which was really the cause? True, Paul had taught that faith in Christ was the way, but now other teachers claiming to believe that Jesus was the Messiah were saying that while observing the law was not enough in itself, it was nonetheless necessary. That teaching perhaps sounded a little strange at first in some of these young churches. It wasn't exactly what Paul had taught them, was it? But soon, this message began to sound more plausible.

It's amazing how opinions begin to seem credible by simple repetition, particularly if the people who advocate them are at all eloquent and earnest; even more, among Christians, if they're known to be personally pious. Perhaps that's how these teachers sounded.

However they gained their hearing, these teachers brought into question the very gospel itself. Christ had died for believers' sins—they were not questioning that. They were not crude self-salvationists. Consider Paul's words: "Grace to you and peace from God our Father and the Lord Jesus Christ, who gave himself for our sins to deliver us from the present evil age, according to the will of our God and Father . . . " (Gal. 1:3–4). I think that the false teachers may have said that they believed this. They may well have affirmed that God is holy and perfect, that he made us in his image, but that we had sinned against him, and that Christ came to live and die and rise again, to bear and bear away God's wrath against us for our sins. But the point they were making had to do with how we are to apprehend Christ and those benefits of his death. Is it by believing? Just believing? Really? Then what about our lives? Do we really want to say that it is merely belief that is the means of obtaining the benefits that Christ has won for us? Or now that we think of it, could it be our repentance? Our changing our way of life? Our adapting our living to God's revealed will? Just what is the principle that describes how we receive the benefits of Christ's salvation? Can it really be simply by faith?

We can imagine how the argument might pick up steam, particularly when the matter of Judaism was added in. Certainly God would not want his ancient people Israel to disappear by assimilation. And what about those special signs that marked off God's people—circumcision, the Sabbath, sacrifices, ritual cleanness rules—surely these signs were to be continued. That would honor God and his Word, wouldn't it? And surely the continuation of these signs would please God and would bring his Spirit's presence to us.

What do you think?

Whatever questions you may have, Paul had no doubt. He called those who were tempted to believe such things "foolish" (Gal. 3:1). The Galatians were in great danger! Paul had preached clearly to them of what Christ had done, but now they seemed to be forgetting exactly that, or misunderstanding it. Paul had preached the crucifixion of Christ among them, and they had presumably partaken of the Lord's Supper. They understood Christ's substitutionary death (which thereby showed that they should have understood the futility of trying to gain salvation by obeying the law).

So Paul asked them a basic question that would send them back to indisputable truth—truth that they themselves had experienced: "Let me ask you only this: Did you receive the Spirit by works of the law or by hearing with faith?" (Gal. 3:2). Paul says, "Choose one of these alternatives."

How do we win with God—how are we justified and declared righteous? How are we freed from sin's grip, from its grim wages and from its just punishment? How are we reconciled with God, and re-established in our relationship with him? These are the questions at the heart of Galatians, and the answer to them gives us, in no small part, the key to the description of the true catholic church.

First, Paul is concerned that all Christian churches everywhere teach how to be forgiven for our sins, or, how to be justified. Granted that we sin, that we do what we should not, and that we do not do what we should, how then on the last day can we hope to win, to be declared righteous by God, the ever-just Judge?

What then is Paul's answer? We win, we are justified, declared righteous, not by observing the law but only by faith in Christ alone. Paul writes, "The life I now live in the flesh I live by faith in the Son of God, who loved me and gave himself for me" (Gal. 2:20; cf. v. 16).

If faith is central, then what is the object of our faith? Paul's answer is clear—Christ and what he has done for us. Paul showed this emphasis early in Galatians, where he spoke of Christ as the One "who gave himself for our sins to deliver us from the present evil age, according to the will of our God and Father" (Gal. 1:3–4). For Paul, Christ is central. We should never think that Paul is teaching that our faith itself is the ground of our justification, the basis of it, the reason for it. The ground of our justification is always and only the work of Jesus Christ. Faith in Christ alone is simply the instrument by which God gives us our justification.

Reflecting on this wonderful truth, John Bunyan wrote in his spiritual autobiography:

> But one day, as I was passing in the field, and that too with some dashes on my conscience, fearing lest yet all was not right, suddenly this sentence fell upon my soul,

"Thy righteousness is in heaven:" and methought withal, I saw, with the eyes of my soul, Jesus Christ at God's right hand; there, I say, is my righteousness; so that wherever I was, or whatever I was adoring, God could not say of me, "He wants [that is, lacks] my righteousness," for that was just before Him. I also saw, moreover, that it was not my good frame of heart that made my righteousness better, nor yet my bad frame that made my righteousness worse; for my righteousness was Jesus Christ himself, the same yesterday, and today, and for ever.[8]

It is not the mere cognitive belief in justification by faith alone that will save you, but rather it is the personal trusting, the "faithing" in Christ alone by which God graciously unites us to Christ, to his suffering, death, and resurrection, and thereby justifies us.

This is Paul's primary concern for all the Christian churches everywhere—that they be sure that justification is only through faith in Christ alone. But there is a second concern that Paul has, on which he wants all Christian churches everywhere to agree, and that is on how we are freed from sin's power. Paul's first concern is with justification—freedom from sin's penalty—and his second concern is with sanctification—freedom from sin's power.

What Paul has to say about sanctification is the same as what he says about justification: Freedom from sin comes not by observing the law, but by faith in Christ alone. Paul writes, "Is the law then contrary to the promises of God? Certainly not! For if a law had been given that could give life, then righteousness would indeed be by the law. But the Scripture imprisoned everything under sin, so that the promise by faith in Jesus Christ might be given to those who believe" (Gal. 3:21–22).

A third aspect of this great truth that Paul presents here, that all truly Christian churches everywhere must agree on, is how we could be adopted as God's children. The false teachers were obviously saying that the way to relate to God is through observing the law. Paul, however, says that this only leads back into servitude. He writes, "How can you turn back again to the weak and worthless elementary principles of the world, whose slaves you want to be once more?" (Gal. 4:9).

The way to have a relationship with God—whoever, whenever, wherever you are—is by faith in Christ alone. Paul says his readers—Jewish and Gentile believers—are all sons of God. We come again to the text that has within it the universal, or catholic, nature of the church:

> For in Christ Jesus you are all sons of God, through faith. For as many of you as were baptized into Christ have put on Christ. There is neither Jew nor Greek, there is neither slave nor free, there is neither male nor female, for you are all one in Christ Jesus. And if you are Christ's, then you are Abraham's offspring, heirs according to promise.
>
> I mean that the heir, as long as he is a child, is no different from a slave, though he is the owner of everything, but he is under guardians and managers until the date set by his father. In the same way we also, when we were children, were enslaved to the elementary principles of the world. But when the fullness of time had come, God sent forth his Son, born of woman, born under the law, to redeem those who were under the law, so that we might receive adoption as sons. And because you are

sons, God has sent the Spirit of his Son into our hearts, crying, "Abba! Father!" So you are no longer a slave, but a son, and if a son, then an heir through God. (Gal. 3:26–4:7)

This is the background to Paul's use of the contrast between Abraham's two sons—one by the free woman, and one by the slave woman, sketched out at the end of chapter 4. We Christians are "like Isaac . . . children of promise" (Gal. 4:28). All Christians—Jewish or Gentile—have been adopted as free sons with full rights.

Paul taught that the Galatian Christians' unity came by means of faith in Christ alone. Note how this unity did not come through the works of the law (see Gal. 2:16). The thrust of Paul's argument in the passage quoted above is from *all sons* in 3:26 to *all one* in 3:28.

This is important because the Galatian teachers were teaching a different way, a distinction between those Galatian Christians who were circumcised and those Galatian Christians who were not circumcised. These false teachers were teaching an identity and a unity based not solely on the faith that they all supposedly shared, but on cultural practices.

In this, the practical importance of the uniqueness of faith begins to appear. There is one way for all people, and that unity reflects the unity of God. Paul argues that all of these Christians together are children of Abraham exactly because they are justified by faith alone (Gal. 3:7). Unity in Christ knows no cultural, class, or gender distinctions. Paul was being emphatic about this. A skeptic could say that he had really gambled his ministry on this very point.

Again, look at Galatians 3:28–29: "There is neither Jew nor Greek, there is neither slave nor free, there is neither male nor female, for you are all one in Christ Jesus. And if you are Christ's, then you are Abraham's offspring, heirs according to promise." The false teachers were trying to introduce another way, which would balkanize the body, and so reflect Christ falsely. Their way would make Christ appear divided when he is not. All of this unifying happened through the One who is the seed of Abraham. The fact that that *offspring* is referred to in the singular in Genesis is Paul's point in Galatians 3:16 and 3:19. Have you noticed Paul's statement in those verses?

> Now the promises were made to Abraham and to his offspring. It does not say, "And to offsprings," referring to many, but referring to one, "And to your offspring," who is Christ . . . Why then the law? It was added because of transgressions, until the offspring should come to whom the promise had been made.

Talk about believing that every word is inspired! Paul believes that a noun being singular rather than plural is of immense significance! Through this one Seed, the promise has come to all who believe.

I wonder if this section surprises you? Did you assume that we are all born children of God? No, friends, we must be adopted. Though we were created by him, we had separated ourselves from him by our sins. The Bible even calls us naturally enemies of God.

But here, in Christ, a way is made for us to be rescued from slavery to sin. And more than that! Isn't it wonderful that God did not simply rescue us from slavery by redeeming us, but that he went further, that he adopted us as sons? Imagine a wealthy man taking a slave youth and not just giving him his freedom, but also making him his son! That and so much more is what God has done for us in Christ!

So we read:

> But when the fullness of time had come, God sent forth his Son, born of woman, born under the law, to redeem those who were under the law, so that we might receive adoption as sons. And because you are sons, God has sent the Spirit of his Son into our hearts, crying, "Abba! Father!" So you are no longer a slave, but a son, and if a son, then an heir through God. (Gal. 4:4–7)

What a privilege! Look again at verse 6: "And because you are sons, God has sent the Spirit of his Son into our hearts, crying, 'Abba! Father!'" This is the other sending. So, God sent his Son into our world, and then he sent "the Spirit of his Son."

How did you imagine that you were accepted into God's family? Did you think it was perhaps by your attendance at church? Turn up enough, and maybe he'll start to know your name? Did you think it was by the growing righteousness of your own life? Friends, we cannot perform ourselves into God's family. Such a glorious adoption comes not by our obeying God's laws, but by trusting in Jesus Christ and his righteousness, whoever we are.

This is what all true Christians everywhere have always believed. This is the truly catholic faith of the truly catholic church.

Some Implications

What are some implications of the church's universality? Understanding the catholicity of the church cuts against some problems in our churches.

Contra provincialism. An understanding of the church's catholicity is a blessing in that it cuts across the mild provincialisms of our world. How many times have we heard in a church the justification for this or that practice with the words, "But we've always done it this way." Paul was calling the Galatians back to the way they had begun—in the very gospel itself. But our traditions are sometimes not as firmly rooted in the very gospel itself. They are often of more recent origin, and more particular to our own country, our own denomination, our own congregation, even our own preferences.

The universal church is not to entrust itself to the will of any one earthly pastor, whether in Rome or elsewhere. While the universal church exists in all cultures, it should be limited to none. The gospel is displayed when Christians of different cultures show themselves all preaching and believing the same gospel.

Some things we take for granted and become wrongly committed to, so that we never submit to the searching examination of Scripture. This is one reason that travel can be useful for a Christian—getting out to discover Christian practices in other places. One of the quickest ways to grow in understanding your own culture is to live in another one. Things that you've always assumed, you begin to realize, are not assumed by others. Is there a correct way? A right answer? Sometimes there is; but sometimes there isn't. It is useful to know what is of the essence of the faith, and what is merely a certain particular expression of it. Understanding the truly catholic nature of the true church works against our provincialism.

Contra sectarianism. From a congregational perspective like my own, denominations are parachurch organizations. But even those of you with a presbyterian or episcopalian polity recognize that your own "church" and its distinctives are not coextensive with the universal church. Therefore, denominations, and those distinctives that separate us from other evangelicals, should never be allowed to become ultimate.

Confessing that there is a catholic church does not mean that denominations are necessarily wrong. Insofar as they allow Christians in conscience to work for the kingdom, and they do not breed an uncharitable and wrongly divisive spirit, they can be helpful (as seen in chapter two on unity). But the recognition of what we hold in common among true, faithful Christians must always be valued more highly and held more deeply than that which divides us.

The gospel is displayed in its essentials when our distinctives are relegated to important but nonessential status. Understanding the truly catholic nature of the true church works against our wrong-headed sectarianism.

Contra racism. This great truth of the universal nature of the true church seriously challenges our uniracial churches. Certainly it disallows churches that only admit people of one race into their membership.

It at least raises questions about the practical segregation that we know in our churches. God forgive our historically Caucasian congregations for any of the ways we have wrongly forbidden or discouraged those of other races from joining us. Also, in America, there is a great story in the African-American churches that were built by our Christian brothers and sisters who knew so much oppression and misery under their Christian "masters." In black churches, black Christians were allowed to exercise leadership and make decisions. From tiny financial means, they built great churches and denominations.

Nevertheless, today, we must say that our racially divided congregations—of any color—do not commend the gospel. Understanding the catholic nature of the Christian church at least raises a question about any church that has a multiracial surrounding population but whose congregation is composed of only one race. Why is this the case? What can been done to better display the fact that the gospel is not limited to just one kind of person? What must we do?

Charles Bridges gives us an excellent image: "The Church is the mirror, that reflects the whole effulgence of the Divine character. It is the grand scene, in which the perfections of Jehovah are displayed to the universe."[9] My friends, this perfect God is not white. And he is not black. He is not Asian, and he is not European. We may need to divide for practicality over language. But, as much as we can, let us not divide our churches for other cultural reasons. The gospel is displayed when those whom the world understands as having no reasons for commonality—who perhaps even have reasons for animosity—stand together united in love.[10] Understanding the truly catholic nature of the truly catholic church works against our racisms.

Contra churches becoming parachurches. Having a ministry to evangelize one particular group of people—for example, college students or businessmen—or to disciple one particular group—mothers of young children or those in the military—is an understandable Christian endeavor. Many Christian parachurch ministries do exactly this. Yet focusing an entire Christian congregation on one particular niche or target group seems to undercut the very universality that the church is to display.

It is entirely appropriate for a group of Christians to band together to work among blue- or white-collar workers, or among skateboarders, or any other countless number of groups by which people identify themselves. But the truly catholic witness of the church to the fact that the gospel is for every kind of person is undermined when we allow such a specific vision or mission statement to focus an entire congregation on only one small part of what a congregation is to be. God in his sovereignty will use various congregations differently; we trust that that is part of his glorious display of himself. But what it is that actually composes any and every congregation does not change, and we should never make the congregation more specific than God does, lest we unwittingly miscommunicate about the universality of God's concern in the gospel.

God's gospel is more greatly magnified when our churches display a greater range of people whom Christ saves by his own mercy. Understanding the truly catholic nature of the truly catholic church undermines our misguided attempts at subjugating God's church to one particular ministry, and so obscuring the comprehensive nature of Christ's mission.

_____

Conclusion

We must see that Christ chooses the living stones who compose his church—that is not our task. And, by God's grace, we can savingly trust in Christ anywhere, any time, regardless of who our parents are. The church's catholicity is rooted in and bounded by the gospel's catholicity. Anytime, anywhere, anyone can be forgiven his or her sins by faith alone in the one and only Savior, our Lord Jesus Christ. That is the true catholic doctrine of the true catholic church. If your church does not teach that, it is not catholic, no matter what's on the sign outside.

5

AN APOSTOLIC CHURCH

PHILIP G. RYKEN

---

*So then you are no longer strangers and aliens, but you
are fellow citizens with the saints and members of the
household of God, built on the foundation of the apostles and prophets, Christ Jesus himself being the cornerstone, in whom the whole structure, being joined
together, grows into a holy temple in the Lord. In him
you also are being built together into a dwelling place
for God by the Spirit. —Ephesians 2:19–22*

We believe in *one* church. There is and there
has only ever been one true communion of
believers united in the Lord Jesus Christ.
We believe in one *holy* church. We have been made holy
by the justifying grace of our Lord Jesus Christ and the
sanctifying work of his Holy Spirit. We believe in one holy
catholic church, a universal, worldwide church united
across time and space. And we believe that this one holy

catholic church is *apostolic*. Or at least this is what we say we believe when we confess our faith using the words of the Nicene Creed.

But what does it mean to be apostolic? It means different things to different Christians. To Roman Catholics—and to some Anglicans—it means that extra-biblical tradition, which is said to go back to the apostles' teaching, has authority for Christians today. It also means that through an "apostolic succession" of bishops in Rome the pope has inherited the apostles' authority—primarily Peter's—and that thus he exercises the rule of Christ over the church.

Charismatics have a different view. For them, the true mark of apostolicity is the exercise of miraculous spiritual gifts, such as healing and tongues. An apostolic church can do today what the apostles did in the early church. When one well-known charismatic leader first became a Christian, he asked his pastor, "When are you going to do the stuff?" "The stuff?" the pastor said. "Yeah, the stuff. You know, like healing the sick and all that stuff they did in the Bible." For charismatics, an apostolic church is one that can "do the stuff" in the twenty-first century.

For still others, being apostolic means getting rid of Christian denominations and starting independent congregations, supposedly like New Testament house churches. But most Protestants—including most evangelicals and Reformed Christians—aren't quite sure *what* it means to be apostolic. Nevertheless, they like the sound of it. The term gives the impression of going back to the beginning, back to the authentic Christianity of the early church.

So what *does* it mean to be an apostolic church, in the true biblical sense of the word? According to the Bible, the church of Jesus Christ is "built on the foundation of the apostles" (Eph. 2:20). Or to read this phrase in its biblical context:

> So then you are no longer strangers and aliens, but you are fellow citizens with the saints and members of the household of God, built on the foundation of the apostles and prophets, Christ Jesus himself being the cornerstone, in whom the whole structure, being joined together, grows into a holy temple in the Lord. In him you also are being built together into a dwelling place for God by the Spirit. (vv. 19–22)

Here we find three overlapping images for the church. The church is a kingdom with citizens drawn from other nations. The church is the household of God—a family of faith. The church is a holy temple in which God dwells by his Spirit. Three images of the church: kingdom, household, temple. But whichever metaphor we choose, the apostles are at the foundation. Everything else is built on them—not just Peter, notice, but all the apostles.

This is an amazing thing for the Bible to say. A building is only as strong as its foundation. So imagine reading only the four gospels, and then hearing God say, "Okay, I'm going to take Peter, Thomas, Andrew, and the rest of the disciples and build my church on their foundation." This is hardly the choice that most people would make. If we admire the apostles, it is because we know what they became by grace, and *not* simply what they were when they started.

Eleven apostles were disciples of Jesus Christ, members of the inner circle of twelve. Then came Matthias, who replaced Judas, and also Paul, the apostle to the Gentiles. As we read about these men in the gospels, the picture that emerges is not very flattering. They were slow to listen, understand, and believe, but quick to miss the point, fall asleep, and run away. To be fair, one of them could walk on water, but only for short distances. And the least promising of all was Paul, who wasn't even a Christian!

The virtue these men most obviously lacked was the one most necessary for ministry, namely, humility. They were always seeking a higher position rather than taking the lowest place. Pillars of the church they were not. And yet they became the foundation of a spiritual building that stands to this very day. Why? What made their ministry foundational for the church? Was it simply the fact that they were the first Christians, or was there something more to it?

We get a hint in Acts 4, where Peter and John are hauled in front of the Sanhedrin for trial. That august body included the most prominent theologians, Bible scholars, and religious leaders of the day. They weren't any more impressed with Peter and John than we would have been. The men on trial were nobodies. They hadn't even been to seminary. Yet they proceeded to make a powerful, articulate defense of the Christian faith. And when the Sanhedrin "saw the boldness of Peter and John, and perceived that they were uneducated, common men, they were astonished. And they recognized that they had been with Jesus" (Acts 4:13).

This is the hint that unravels the mystery of the apostolic foundation for the church: *these men had been with Jesus*. Whatever was distinctive about them, whatever set them apart, whatever gave their ministry its abiding significance, it was all because of their relationship with Jesus. This explained their message and their mission. And it explains why to this day, the church is built on their foundation. The apostles had been with Jesus.

Christ-Centered Preaching

What are the hallmarks of apostolicity? As we survey the New Testament, looking at the apostles and their ministry, what do we learn about what it means to be an apostolic church?

First, we see that they were *Christ-centered in their preaching*. We see this clearly in Ephesians, where the church is said to be "built on the foundation of the apostles and the prophets, Christ Jesus himself being the cornerstone" (Eph. 2:20; cf. Ps. 118:22; Isa. 28:16; 1 Pet. 2:6–7). For any building there is something even more fundamental than its foundation, namely, the cornerstone. The cornerstone is what keeps a building on the square. It fixes the angle and sets the lines for the rest of the structure, starting with the foundation, which the cornerstone holds together. Jesus is the cornerstone, and the way that the apostles founded the church was by lining up with him.

The apostolic connection to Christ is inherent in the name "apostle." An apostle is an official representative who is commissioned to carry a message or to perform an official duty. The word is closely related to the Hebrew term *shaliach*. At the time of Christ, a *shaliach* was someone in the Jewish community who acted as an official representative—of the Sanhedrin, for example. By virtue of his commission, a *shaliach* had the authority to speak for someone else.

To give an analogy, this is like a father sending a child to tell his siblings that it is time for dinner. The child who is sent with the message is speaking on his father's behalf. Among other things, that means that if the rest of them don't come right away, they will have to answer to their father. By failing to obey the messenger's summons, they are showing disrespect to their father. Jesus said something similar about his apostles. He said that whoever received them was receiving him, and whoever rejected them was rejecting him (Matt. 10:40).

A *shaliach* also had the power to act for another. He had something like the power of attorney that authorizes someone to sign legal documents, or like the authority of a foreign diplomat who is empowered to sign a treaty. The apostles did something similar for Jesus. They spoke for him, broadcasting his saving message to the world. And they acted for him, baptizing, discipling, teaching, and performing miracles. The apostles were fully commissioned to speak and to act for Jesus as his representatives in the world.

This apostolic authority helps explain the puzzling comment at the beginning of Acts, where Luke tells us that in his former book—that is to say, the Gospel of Luke—he "dealt with all that Jesus *began* to do and teach, until the day when he was taken up" (Acts 1:1–2). What is puzzling is the implication that Jesus had more to do and say after he ascended to heaven. Yet Jesus does and says almost nothing in Acts. In fact, people usually call the book "The Acts of the Apostles." So why would Luke say that his gospel was only the beginning of what Jesus said and did?

Luke proceeds to explain: "In the first book . . . I have dealt with all that Jesus began to do and teach, until the day when he was taken up, after he had given commands through the Holy Spirit to the apostles whom he had chosen" (Acts 1:1–2). This is the answer. Jesus had more to say and do, but his plan was to say it and do it by his Spirit working through his apostles. They were the ones who were fully authorized to speak and to act in his name. This is what it meant to be an apostle.

What did the apostles say? What did they do? They preached the gospel, announcing the good news of the cross and the empty tomb. Jesus said to them, "You will be my witnesses in Jerusalem and in all Judea and Samaria, and to the end of the earth" (Acts 1:8). Jesus was sending the apostles out as his representatives, his messengers, his *shaliachs* to the world. They were commissioned to bear witness to his saving work, testifying to what they had seen: his crucifixion and his resurrection.

We see this again and again all the way through Acts. We see it in chapter 2, when Peter preached on the Day of Pentecost. What did he preach? The cross and the empty tomb. He reminded people how only weeks before, Jesus of Nazareth had been crucified. Then he said, "This Jesus God raised up, and of that we are all witnesses . . . Know for certain that God has made him both Lord and Christ, this Jesus whom you crucified" (Acts 2:32, 36). We find Peter preaching the same message in chapter 3. This time he was in Solomon's portico, explaining how he had the power to heal a man who was lame. He told people, "You killed the Author of life, whom God raised from the dead. To this we are witnesses" (Acts 3:15). Once again, Peter was witnessing to the death and resurrection of Jesus. On each occasion, he preached the cross and the empty tomb.

In chapter 4 he preached the same sermon again (the way preachers do), this time to the Sanhedrin. He said, "Let it be known to all of you . . . that by the name of Jesus Christ of Nazareth, whom you crucified, whom God raised from the dead—by him this man is standing before you well. This Jesus is the stone that was rejected by you, the builders, which has become the cornerstone" (Acts 4:10–11). Peter was explaining the basis for his apostolic authority. What right did he have to heal anybody? He was doing it in the name of Jesus. He was lining himself up with Jesus, the cornerstone. And he was doing it so that people would know Jesus as crucified Savior and risen Lord.

Or consider Acts 10, where Peter begins to preach the gospel to the Gentiles. New audience, same message: "And we are witnesses . . . They put him [Jesus] to death by hanging him on a tree, but God raised him on the third day and made him to appear, not to all the people but to us who had been chosen by God as witnesses . . . And he commanded us to preach to the people . . . forgiveness of sins through his name" (Acts 10:39–43). Once again, Peter was witnessing to the cross and the empty tomb.

It wasn't just Peter, either. When the apostle Paul started preaching, he used the same sermon outline. In his sermon at Pisidian Antioch he said, "Brothers . . . to us has been sent the message of this salvation"(Acts 13:26). What was this message?

> Though they found in him [Jesus] no guilt worthy of death, they asked Pilate to have him executed. And when they had carried out all that was written of him, they took him down from the tree and laid him in a tomb. But God raised him from the dead, and for many days he appeared to those who . . . are now his witnesses to the people. (Acts 13:28–31)

Here we see the same pattern: death, resurrection, witness. Or again in chapter 17, the Bible tells how Paul preached to the Thessalonians, "explaining and proving that it was necessary for the Christ to suffer and to rise from the dead" (Acts 17:3).

The apostles always stayed on message. This is true all the way through the New Testament. They were always preaching Christ—his substitutionary atonement and his bodily resurrection. This is the distinguishing mark of true apostolicity. An apostolic church, therefore, is one that preaches the gospel the apostles preached—the gospel of the cross and the empty tomb. In the words of Edmund Clowney, "The sure sign of Christ's true church is the preaching of the apostolic gospel."[1] An apostolic church preaches Jesus Christ. It preaches his genuine deity and true humanity. It preaches him as God the Son, the Second Person of the Trinity. It preaches him in his sinless life, his atoning death, and his glorious resurrection.

This is why the apostles were always warning people not to teach or to believe any other gospel. A church that preaches any other gospel is no church at all. For a church to be a church it has to preach the gospel. It can struggle in all kinds of ways—like most churches in the New Testament—and still be apostolic, *if* it has the gospel.

I praise God that when he made me a preacher, he gave me a gospel to preach. And I praise God that it's the same gospel that James Boice preached during the years he preceded me at Tenth Presbyterian Church, which was the same gospel that Jonathan Edwards, John Calvin, and Augustine preached. It is the same gospel they all preached because it is the gospel that Peter, Paul, and all the apostles preached—the gospel of the crucified and risen Christ. This is the gospel that the church needs today. Not a new gospel. Not a different gospel. But the same old gospel of Jesus, which is the only gospel there is. Anyone who believes this gospel is an apostolic Christian, built on the foundation of the apostles.

Bible-Based Teaching

The apostles preached the gospel of Jesus Christ from the Scriptures. This is a second mark of apostolicity. An apostolic church is *Bible-based in its teaching*. There is a clue about this in Ephesians 2, where the church is said to be "built on the foundation of the apostles and prophets" (v. 20).

The first thing to decide about this verse is who the prophets are. Naturally we think first of the Old Testament prophets: Isaiah, Jeremiah, and all the rest. This may be the right interpretation. If so, then the reason Paul starts with the apostles is because they are the ones who preach Christ most clearly and directly. We come to know

Christ through their message. But Paul may be referring to the prophets he mentions in Ephesians. These men "received and proclaimed direct messages from God and worked along with the apostles in the early days" of the Christian church, before the New Testament was completed[2] (see Eph. 3:5; 4:11). Like the apostles, they spoke for God.

Whether or not Paul is referring here to the Old Testament prophets, we should recognize that when the apostles established the foundation for the church, they used building stones quarried from the Old Testament. When they preached Christ, they invariably did it by quoting from the prophets. This was true of their sermons in Acts. When Peter preached at Pentecost, he took Joel 2 and Psalm 16 for his texts. He did something similar at Solomon's portico. He preached the God of Abraham, Isaac, and Jacob, saying, "What God foretold by the mouth of all the prophets, that his Christ would suffer, he thus fulfilled" (Acts 3:18). He quoted from Moses. He referred to Samuel. He argued on the basis of the covenant God made with Abraham. Even when Peter preached to Cornelius, the Gentile, he used themes and phrases from the Old Testament, and then ended by saying, "To him all the prophets bear witness that everyone who believes in him receives forgiveness of sins through his name" (Acts 10:43).

Paul preached the same way, of course. In his sermon at Pisidian Antioch he rehearsed the story line of the Old Testament, quoting from Psalm 2, Isaiah 55, Psalm 16, Habakkuk 1, and Isaiah 42. Similarly, when he preached in Thessalonica, explaining and proving the death and resurrection of Christ, he did so "from the Scriptures" (Acts 17:2), meaning the Old Testament. We find this everywhere we turn in the New Testament. The apostles seemingly were incapable of writing more than a few sentences without quoting something from the prophets, telling a story from the Old Testament, or referring to some event in the history of salvation. According to Professor Andrew Hill of Wheaton College, of the almost 8,000 verses in the New Testament, more than 2,500 either quote or allude to something from the Old Testament.[3]

This is one hallmark of apostolicity. An apostolic church is Bible-based in its teaching—both testaments. An apostolic church is not simply a New Testament church; it is also an Old Testament church. It is a church that preaches Christ from the Old Testament Scriptures, as the apostles did. This is the way the apostles preached because it is the way Jesus taught them to preach. On the road to Emmaus, Jesus started lecturing his disciples on Old Testament christology: "And beginning with Moses and all the Prophets, he interpreted to them in all the Scriptures the things concerning himself" (Luke 24:27). Don't you wish you had the tape from *that* sermon? But in a way, we do have the tape, because the apostles were always preaching the gospel according to the prophets. Where did they learn how to do this? They learned it from Jesus, of course, and to this day we interpret the Old Testament the way they did.

An apostolic church also teaches the New Testament, because this is where we find the apostolic message itself. We do not hear their message by reading extra-biblical literature that supposedly comes from one of the apostles, by relying on the church's oral tradition, or by listening to someone who claims to be a twenty-first-century apostle. The way we get the apostolic message today is by reading the New Testament.

The apostles expected believers to receive what they wrote as the Word of God. For example, when Paul wrote a letter to a church, he expected people in other churches to read it too, and to recognize its apostolic authority (see Col. 4:16; 1 Thess. 5:27). It is clear from what Peter says that he also regarded Paul's writings as having binding authority for the church (see 2 Peter 3:2). These men were *shaliachs*—men sent to speak for Jesus. And what enabled them to speak with such authority was the inspiration of the Holy Spirit. Jesus promised them, "When the Helper comes, whom I will send to you from the Father, the Spirit of truth . . . he will bear witness about me. And you also will bear witness" (John 15:26–27; cf. 16:13–15). The witness of the apostles was the witness of the Holy Spirit to Christ. This is why the apostolic writings come to us with the full authority of Almighty God, as the church has recognized from its earliest days.

The apostolic testimony is final. A building has only one foundation, and once it is laid, no other foundation can be established. Edmund Clowney writes: "New Testament revelation is part of Christ's work through his Spirit; it is the apostolic foundation on which Christ builds his church. The gospel witness that Christ gives through his apostles is not repeated, nor is their written testimony to be amended."[4]

The apostles' ministry was once and for all. The reason for this is obvious. To be an apostle, a man had to be an eyewitness to the resurrection. This could only be true of the original apostles and not of anyone who followed after them. Therefore, "As direct witnesses and messengers of the risen Lord, the apostles can have no successors . . . Apostleship . . . died out with the death of the last apostle."[5] But the apostolic message still speaks from the pages of the New Testament. This is our foundation.

By Grace, through Faith, for God's Glory

An apostolic church is a Christ-preaching, Bible-teaching church. Several other marks of apostolicity also need to be mentioned. One is grace. An apostolic church is *grace-dependent in its ministry.*

The gospel that the apostles preached was always a gospel of grace. It was good news for people who didn't deserve any good news because all they deserved was to be judged and condemned for their sin. This is Paul's argument in Ephesians 2. He begins with the reminder that once we were dead in our trespasses and sins, and that because of our disobedience we were under the wrath of God. "But God," he writes in verse 4, making a divine interruption, made us alive in Christ. When we were spiritually dead and thus unable to save ourselves, God gave us new spiritual life. This is grace. It is something we could never accomplish and don't even deserve. By grace we have been saved (Eph. 2:5, 8).

The apostles were always speaking of grace. This was partly because they were so painfully aware of the depth of their own depravity. We see this in Peter, who confessed, "I am a sinful man, O Lord" (Luke 5:8). And we see it in Paul, who described himself as the worst of sinners (e.g., 1 Tim. 1:15). The apostles knew that they could not save themselves. However, they also knew that God had grace for them in Christ. As Peter said, "We believe that we will be saved through the grace of the Lord Jesus" (Acts 15:11). And this same grace was at work in their ministry, which Paul described as one of "testify[ing] to the gospel of the grace of God" (Acts 20:24). He also said, "by the grace of God I am what I am, and his grace toward me was not in vain . . . [I]t was not I, but the grace of God that is with me" (1 Cor. 15:10). Whatever the apostles accomplished in ministry was entirely due to the grace of God.

The way to receive this grace is by faith. God's grace is not something that can be earned. If it could be earned, then it wouldn't be grace. Instead, the gospel is something we believe. When the apostles preached the gospel, they always told people what Jesus accomplished through his crucifixion and resurrection. But they didn't just stop there, as if all people needed to know were the facts of salvation. They always called people to put their faith in Christ. They told them to trust in the crucified and risen Christ for their salvation. An apostolic church—and this is a fourth mark of apostolicity—is *faith-seeking in its evangelism*.

We see this in the way that the apostles preached. Consider again some of the sermons from Acts. When Peter preached on Solomon's Portico, he called people to "the faith that is through Jesus" (Acts 3:16), and "many of those who had heard the word believed" (Acts 4:4). Or take Peter's sermon to Cornelius, which he ended by saying, "To him [Jesus] all the prophets bear witness that everyone who believes in him receives forgiveness of sins through his name" (Acts 10:43). Or again at Pisidian Antioch, after Paul had carefully worked his way through the story of salvation, culminating with the resurrection of

Jesus Christ, he said, "through this man forgiveness of sins is proclaimed to you, and by him everyone who believes is freed" (Acts 13:38).

The key word in each case is "believe." The apostles always called people to put their faith in Jesus. The gospel that they preached—the gospel of Jesus Christ, the gospel of the cross and the empty tomb, the gospel foretold by the prophets, the gracious gospel that comes from God—is a gospel to be believed. It is a gospel that saves by grace through faith: "For by grace you have been saved through faith. And this is not your own doing; it is the gift of God, not a result of works, so that no one may boast" (Eph. 2:8–9).

The word "boast" reminds us why the apostles preached this way. The reason they said that salvation comes by faith and not by works and the reason they insisted that it is a gift of grace rather than a reward of merit is that they wanted God to get the glory. This was their apostolic motivation. They were absolutely determined that God should get all the credit that he deserved. They were not preaching to enhance their own reputation; they were preaching for the glory of God. Thus we can add a fifth mark of apostolicity to our list: An apostolic church is *God-glorifying in its vision*. We want to give all the glory to God.

This is what God wants as well. Indeed, it is the reason he is building his church on the foundation of the apostles. He wants to be glorified. After explaining that Jesus Christ is the cornerstone, Paul went on to say, "in whom the whole structure, being joined together, grows into a holy temple in the Lord. In him you also are being built together into a dwelling place for God by the Spirit"

(Eph. 2:21–22). This verse summarizes many of the things we are saying about the church in this book. It is one church, in which we are all joined together in Christ. It is a holy church—a holy temple for God. It is an apostolic church, built on the foundation of the apostles. And it is all these things for the glory of God. A temple is a holy place for God to fill with his presence so that people will see his glory.

At the end of Ephesians 2, therefore, we see the plan of the Triune God to reveal his glory in the church. The Son is the cornerstone; the Spirit is the builder; the Father is the resident. With this in mind, Paul proceeds in the next chapter to give this stirring doxology: "To him be glory in the church and in Christ Jesus throughout all generations, forever and ever. Amen" (Eph. 3:21). This was the chief end of the apostles, and also the chief end of the church: to glorify God and enjoy him forever.

The Apostolic Reformation

There are many other things we could say about what it means to be an apostolic church. But for now we must be content with identifying five marks of apostolicity. An apostolic church is Christ-centered in its preaching, Bible-based in its teaching, grace-dependent in its ministry, faith-seeking in its evangelism, and God-glorifying in its vision.

As we review this list, something about it ought to seem familiar: Christ, Scripture, grace, faith, glory. These are the Protestant Reformation doctrines: Christ alone, Scripture alone, grace alone, faith alone, and to God alone be the glory! This is not surprising. When men like Martin Luther and John Calvin started to reform the church, they deliberately went back to the apostles for their theology and their practice. They were not trying to start anything new; they were simply trying to build the church back up on its proper foundations. Here is how theologian Paul Althaus has summarized Martin Luther's view of the apostles: "Since the apostles are the foundation of the church, their authority is basic. No other authority can be equal to theirs. Every other authority in the church is derived from following the teaching of the apostles and is validated only by its conformity to their teaching."[6]

The Reformers did this in each of the five areas we have mentioned. They did it with Jesus Christ. Over against those who were adding human effort to the finished work of Christ, they said that we have salvation in Christ alone. They did the same thing with Scripture. Many in the church were treating tradition as an equal authority with God's Word. But the Reformers said that Scripture alone is our ultimate authority for faith and practice. The Reformers did the same thing with grace and faith. People were adding works to faith as the basis for their standing before God; justification was no longer a pure gift of grace. But the Reformers insisted that salvation is by grace alone, through faith alone, in Christ alone.

The Reformers said all this out of a holy zeal for God and his glory. They recognized that people were building on the wrong foundation. The emphasis was on human tradition and human effort—what people can do to get right with God. But the Reformers wanted to preserve all the glory for God. They wanted him to be glorified in his Word and in the grace of saving faith. Like the apostles, they said that salvation was all of God, so that God alone would get all the glory.

The Apostolic Church in the Twenty-First Century

Although it has taken a while to get here, the point I wish to make is very simple: the Reformers emphasized Christ alone, Scripture alone, grace alone, and faith alone because they believed in the apostolic church. Their perspective is sometimes called Reformation theology. It is certainly the theology that the Reformers taught. We may also call it apostolic Christianity, for it is what the apostles taught as well. We do not have to call it anything at all. We can simply say that it is plain old biblical sense. But no matter what we call it, it is the theology that the church desperately needs today.

Notice the tense of the verb that Paul uses in Ephesians 2, where he says, "In him [Christ] you also *are being built together* into a dwelling place for God by the Spirit" (v. 22). The verb for building (*synoikodomeisthe*) is a present participle. It describes something that is happening right now, on an ongoing basis. God is building us together. We are being built into a holy temple, a dwelling place for God. The church is not a static building, but a living, growing community that is still under construction. How is it being built? To this day, the one, true, holy catholic church is being built on the foundation of the apostles.

We are living at a time when the foundation is under attack. It is not the superstructure of the Christian faith that is being attacked—things on the periphery of Chris-

111

tian doctrine—but its very foundation. Each of the five hallmarks of apostolicity is under pressure in the evangelical church as much as anywhere else. And if the foundation is shaken, how can the building stand?

There is an attack on Christ. Under the influence of other world religions, many people say that Jesus Christ is *not* the only way to God, that sinners can be saved without trusting in his death on the cross for their sins. At the same time, there are many attacks on Scripture. New Bible translations are taking us farther and farther away from the words of God. There is a relentless attack on the inerrancy of Scripture from scholars who think that the Bible is limited by time and place. And there is an appalling lack of biblical literacy, in part because so many churches have given up teaching the Bible with any seriousness.

Then there is an attack on grace, as there always is. We are legalists by nature, so we are always trying to work our way to God's blessing. Today we see it in all the man-centered methods people use for evangelism and church growth. There is also an attack on faith, as many evangelicals and even some Reformed theologians downplay the doctrine of justification by faith alone. Some are saying that there is little or nothing wrong with Roman Catholic teaching on this point. Others are embracing a new perspective on Paul and the law that denies the imputation of Christ's righteousness. There are even attacks on God's glory, especially in our worship, which all too often is more egocentric than theocentric. Then there is the dangerous new doctrine of open theism, which says that God does not know the future, but is only working things out as he goes along.

The people making these attacks usually claim that the church is in a new situation that requires new methods, even a new theology. There are many problems with this way of thinking, but perhaps the most obvious is that God has not done anything new. The last big event in salvation history was sending his Son to suffer and to die for our sins. This is still the foundation for the church today: the full and final salvation that God has provided in Jesus Christ. What we need, therefore, is not something new and supposedly up-to-date—a new theology or methodology. What we need is apostolic Christianity.

We need to defend the true doctrine of Christ. Like the apostles, we believe that Jesus is the only way to God, that there is no other name under heaven by which we must be saved (Acts 4:12). And once we understand the gospel, we can see why. The gospel says that God the very Son died on the cross for sinners and that he was raised from the dead to give eternal life. Who else has done *that?* No one else, which is why only Jesus can save us from our sins.

We need to maintain our commitment to Scripture. Today there is such widespread biblical ignorance that even people who have been going to church for years need to be taught the basics for the very first time. Over against all the relativistic thinking of our age, we defend the Bible as the inerrant, infallible, and authoritative Word of God. And because it is the Word of God, we read it, meditate on it, memorize it, study it, and teach it to others.

We are called to be grace-dependent in our ministry. We always need to be reminded of this, because we so easily slip back into a performance-based approach to Christianity. We measure our spiritual success by what

God has done for us in Christ, rather than by what we do for God. We are also called to do ministry God's way, trusting him to use his Word to do the real work, rather than coming up with our own ways of "doing church." And we are called to keep inviting people to faith, telling them to stop trusting in their own righteousness and start trusting in Christ alone, so that God will forgive their sins and grant them the gift of imputed righteousness.

In all these things we give the glory to God. At a time when there is so much triviality in Christian worship, we want to give God our very best. Rather than settling for the diminished deity of open theism, we praise the infinite, omniscient, omnipotent sovereignty of Almighty God.

There are many reasons why the church must keep building on its apostolic foundation, but one of the most important is that the salvation of sinners depends on it. This truth was driven home for me as I watched a young woman come to faith in Jesus Christ. She first came to church with a friend. When she was asked about her relationship with Jesus Christ, it quickly became apparent that she was from a different theological tradition, one that promotes salvation by works and not by faith alone. She and her friend were asked a serious question: "If you were to die tonight and stand before God, and if he were to ask you, 'Why should I let you into my heaven?' what would you say?" The woman basically said that she had received the sacraments, and that although she knew she wasn't perfect, she had tried to be a good person all her life. Her friend's answer was very different. He said his only hope was that Jesus Christ died for his sins on the cross.

When they were both finished, the young woman said, "Wow, those answers were completely different!"

Even though she was not yet a Christian, she could see that there was an eternity of difference between asking God to accept her on her own merits and asking him to let what Jesus did count for her. Not long afterwards the Holy Spirit brought her to saving faith in Jesus Christ.

As she reflected on her conversion, the woman lamented that in all her years of going to church, no one had ever given her the gospel. No one had taught her the Old and New Testaments. No one had explained to her the imputation of Christ's righteousness. She didn't know about the free gift of God's grace; she thought it was up to her to be good enough for God. She didn't know what it meant to put her faith in Christ alone for salvation. And as a result, she hadn't been living for the glory of God.

When I heard what she said, at first it made me angry. How could somebody take spiritual responsibility for precious souls and never tell people what they needed to know to be saved? But I realized that I shouldn't be angry—just sad—and more committed than ever to building the church on the right foundation. I praise God that the woman eventually came to a church where she heard the gospel preached from the Scriptures, and where she was saved by grace through faith in the crucified and risen Christ, so that now she can glorify God forever. I praise God for all this because I believe in the apostolic church, the church that is being "built on the foundation of the apostles and prophets, Christ Jesus himself being the cornerstone" (Eph. 2:20).

6

EPILOGUE: CHRIST AND HIS CHURCH

RICHARD D. PHILLIPS

[God] seated him at his right hand in the heavenly places, far above all rule and authority and power and dominion, and above every name that is named, not only in this age but also in the one to come. And he put all things under his feet and gave him as head over all things to the church, which is his body, the fullness of him who fills all in all. —Ephesians 1:20–23

In the previous four chapters, we have examined the classic description of the Christian church as rendered by the Nicene Creed. The church is one, holy, catholic, and apostolic. Realizing and understanding these things will help us to recover the church's identity, which we believe has been lost or discarded by many in recent years.

117

It is, however, the authors' conviction that for all the glory of the church, despite her unity, holiness, catholicity, and apostolicity, she is nothing without her Lord Jesus Christ. Like a bride standing alone at the altar, the church without Christ is at best an exercise in play-acting and at worst a fraud.

It is for this reason that we begin and end this study of the church by reflection on her union with Jesus Christ.

As prologue, we examined the origin of the church in her great profession of faith in Christ, to which our Lord gave a promise of his building the church and a prophecy of her victory, even against the very gates of hell. There, too, at the beginning, we saw the principle of the cross, which all through the church's history governs her death to sin and resurrection to eternal life with Christ.

Now we conclude our study of the church by considering her future destiny in union with Christ. For this, we turn to the end of Ephesians 1, a most carefully organized chapter that serves as introduction to this epistle, which focuses so greatly on Christ and his church.

Ephesians 1 begins with a typical opening greeting from Paul. The rest of the chapter consists of two long sentences. The first is a hymn of praise for the blessings of God in our salvation in Christ. The second is a prayer of thanks and petition to God for his readers, as is found at the beginning of most of Paul's letters. In these two sections of Ephesians 1, Paul deftly introduces the themes he is going to develop later in the letter: the plan of salvation, the sovereignty of God, the nature and destiny of a Christian, and the coordinated roles of the members of the divine Trinity in salvation.

Given the care of Paul's construction, the note he chooses to strike at the chapter's end is undoubtedly significant. Here we encounter the theme that rises above the others and in which they are tied together, namely the church's union with the crucified, risen, and exalted Christ.

Christ Exalted

Paul ends this chapter with the same theme on which the Gospel accounts end, the ascension and exaltation of Jesus Christ. Forty days after his resurrection, Jesus was taken up before the disciples, visibly rising into heaven as the Shekinah glory cloud enfolded him. Thus was his earthly ministry concluded and his heavenly reign begun.

The exaltation of Christ is God's ultimate vindication of our Lord. Remember the scene as Jesus was dying on the cross. The religious leaders mocked, "He trusts in God; let God deliver him now, if he desires him. For he said, 'I am the Son of God'" (Matt. 27:43). Here is God's reply. Christ's resurrection and ascension prove beyond a doubt that God accepted Christ's obedient life and especially his death as the sacrifice for our sins. The world despised him, but God exalted him to the highest place, proving that his claims were all true.

Paul presents Christ's exaltation in two terms, first in terms of his *exalted dignity*. He writes that God "seated him at his right hand in the heavenly places, far above all rule and authority and power and dominion, and above every name that is named, not only in this age but also in the one to come" (Eph. 1:20–21).

119

Jesus is portrayed as *seated* at the place of honor in heaven. Christians have long understood this to indicate his finished work as our Savior. The writer to the Hebrews reports, "After making purification for sins, he sat down at the right hand of the Majesty on high" (Heb. 1:3). This contrasts with the Jewish priests who never sat down in the temple: "Every priest stands daily at his service, offering repeatedly the same sacrifices, which can never take away sins" (Heb. 10:11). But because Jesus' sacrificial death perfectly satisfied God's justice, God exalted him to sit in the heavenly sanctuary.

Furthermore, sitting denotes the dignity that Jesus shares with God. All others stand in God's presence, but Jesus sits with him on the throne. By sitting, Jesus shows that his position and reign are firmly established. This is what Daniel saw in his vision of the "one like a son of man" who "came to the Ancient of Days and was presented before him. And to him was given dominion and glory and a kingdom . . . his dominion is an everlasting dominion, which shall not pass away, and his kingdom one that shall not be destroyed" (Dan. 7:13–14).

The writer of Hebrews points out how this shows Christ's *supremacy to the angels,* in that he became "as much superior to the angels as the name he has inherited is more excellent than theirs" (Heb. 1:4). Paul makes this same point, placing Jesus "far above all rule and authority and power and dominion, and above every name that is named, not only in this age but also in the one to come" (Eph. 1:21). These are designations for spiritual beings. Many commentators see these as different grades and ranks within an angelic hierarchy, although speculation on that matter is not Paul's emphasis. I think it could also be Paul's habit of piling on terms when he really wants to make a point. Here, he brings forth every word in current usage for a spiritual power, and he places Christ above them all.

Paul is probably also reacting against a superstitious idea current in the area at that time, that angels and other semidivine spirits have to be placated before we can get to God. This was an early form of what would later be called Gnosticism. Paul's letter to the Colossians, which he sent along with Ephesians, shows his concern about this. In this case, Paul is pointing out that since Christ is exalted over all, any such ideas must fall away before his supremacy. Furthermore, Ephesus was a center of pagan magical activity in which sorcerers evoked "names" or "titles" of various powers. But all these ideas are countered by the exaltation of Christ, to whom believers have access by simple faith. Whatever title or name one can think of, either now or in the future, it pales before the status and honor and privilege given to Christ. He is "far above . . . every name that is named, not only in this age but also in the one to come" (Eph. 1:21).

Moreover, Jesus is seated *at God's right hand*. Kings place someone at their right hand to grant honor and to show participation in their rule. This is the highest dignity that heaven itself can afford, and such a place is granted to our Lord Jesus Christ. We have here the fulfillment of Old Testament Scripture, which the apostles often used as a proof of Christ's divinity and lordship: "The LORD says to my Lord: 'Sit at my right hand, until I make your enemies your footstool'" (Ps. 110:1).

Such is the exalted *dignity* of Christ in heaven. But Paul also wants us to know that Christ is exalted in his present *dominion*. It is not merely honor that Jesus has received but also royal authority. This is an implication of his sitting at God's right hand. Paul adds, "And [God] put all things under his feet" (Eph. 1:22).

All these rulers and authorities, powers and lords—many of whom may have been threatening to the Christians in that pagan age—are not only inferior to Christ but they are subject to him. The imagery reminds us of Joshua's victory over the five Amorite kings. After their defeat, Joshua brought forth the five chieftains. Calling his generals, he said, "Come near; put your feet on the necks of these kings" (Josh. 10:24). It was a sign of their complete subjugation to his power and was a prelude to their execution.

That is the situation of every hostile power, circumstance, and danger to which we are exposed—they are under Christ's feet, all our enemies soon to be put away. Just as Jesus' voice stilled the storm on the lake, just as his presence caused the demons to grovel in terror, likewise there is no threat to us that does not bow down in his presence or is able to evade the power of his sovereign will.

This is what Jesus declared before his ascension: "All authority in heaven and on earth has been given to me" (Matt. 28:18). We need to remember this in a time when Christ's reign is mainly associated with his second coming. But he is reigning now over the universe. He is glorified now; he wears the crown even as we gather in our churches, no less than he will in the day of his glorious return. The power that raised him, that delivered him from the agony of the cross to the triumph of his exaltation in honor and dominion, is the same power that is lifting us from our sins and from the grip of this evil world so that we might follow Jesus and join him where he is.

Christ Exalted for the Church

Paul is directing our attention to the exalted station of Christ so that we will trust and honor him, and that we will understand all that it means to be joined to him in faith. To this end he adds that God "gave him as head over all things to the church, which is his body" (Eph. 1:22–23). Paul's first point is that Jesus is exalted over all—his and our enemies are under his feet. His second point is that the exalted Christ is given to the church as its head, ruling on its behalf, while the church is given to him as his body.

Paul uses many metaphors to describe the rich and complex relationship between Christ and his people. In our last chapter we studied Paul's teaching in Ephesians 2, where he describes us as God's kingdom and household, and also as a temple that God is erecting on the firm, apostolic foundation. Later, in Ephesians 5, Paul says that the union of a husband and wife illustrates the mystery of our union with Christ.

But the chief designation Paul employs is that of a head and its body. This points to the organic union between Christ and his church. A human being is not just a collection of parts but an integrated whole. Such is our spiritual union with Christ. The head and the body are one, inseparable. Paul also has in mind Christ's ruling or governing function over the church, in the same way that the head rules the body.

Unlike Christ's enemies, whom he rules by force, we are ruled in the way the head governs the body. His rule is not on us but within us. This tells us, by the way, that we must reject all schemes that place a human leader atop the church, as with the Roman Catholic Church and the pope. The church has only one head, who lives and reigns forever, Jesus Christ himself.

Finally, Paul's metaphor suggests that the head is the source of life and vitality for the body, just as the brain's nervous system conveys energy and activity to the various body parts. Jesus made this point, comparing himself to a vine that gives life to the branches. "Apart from me," he explained, "you can do nothing" (John 15:5).

In this context Paul makes an amazing statement that shows why all this matters for us. Some translations blur this, such as the New International Version, which says here that God "appointed him to be head over everything for the church." Literally, however, it reads, "God *gave* him as head over all things *to* the church." This Jesus, exalted in dignity and dominion, with all things under his feet and all glory attached to his throne, is given by God to us the church. And what a gift he is! I want to point out three things this means by way of application.

First, this is a great proof of *the assurance of our salvation* if we are in Christ. Jesus Christ is enthroned forever above all powers and dominions at the right hand of God. It is a man, a human being, who sits upon that throne. He is inseparably joined to us as the head to his body. Our salvation, then, is utterly assured. We are like Joseph's brothers, who came to Egypt only to find their long-lost brother enthroned over the mighty foreign land. That is what we shall find in heaven, that the one who gave himself for us is seated in the place of honor and power. He sits enthroned in a human body marked by the wounds he suffered for us. This proves that our sins are put away forever and that we who trust in him will certainly find a place with him there.

Furthermore, he has conquered our every foe. In his death and resurrection and ascension he has subdued all his foes and ours, including sin, the world, the devil, and death. We may now face all of these without fear. Yes, we must still contend with these enemies, with people and powers that tempt and afflict and oppose us. But they are enemies he has already subdued. Our present conflict is with defeated foes. Instead of truly threatening our salvation, they are rather instruments of sanctification and growth, enemies Christ allows only to go far enough to do us good in our struggles as we learn to trust in him. "In this world you will have trouble," he told the disciples. "But take heart! I have overcome the world!" (John 16:33)

Our second application is to understand *the power that is available to us* because Christ is exalted. God gave him as head over everything to the church. Therefore what aid could we need that is beyond his ability to give? What obstacle is so great that he cannot remove it? What calling have we received that he cannot supply the power to fulfill? What challenge do you have, what temptation or trial do you face, with what sin are you burdened but that Christ cannot overcome it as he works in you with his almighty power? If we realize this, what peace we will have, what power and confidence in prayer! Christ our Lord is enthroned in heaven and his power is available to us.

The great illustration of this truth is the apostle Paul himself. Who was the man who wrote this superb letter? He was the greatest sinner in all the world, the harshest critic and most hateful opponent of Christians. But how easy it was for Christ to turn this man into the great apostle of grace, the man who did more to establish the early church than anyone else! Christ changed his mind, changed his heart, changed his life. Paul, then named Saul of Tarsus, was traveling to Damascus to persecute the Christians there, having worn out the Christians in Jerusalem and needing fresh victims. Luke tells us what happened:

> Now as he went on his way, he approached Damascus, and suddenly a light from heaven flashed around him. And falling to the ground he heard a voice saying to him, "Saul, Saul, why are you persecuting me?" And he said, "Who are you, Lord?" And he said, "I am Jesus, whom you are persecuting. But rise and enter the city, and you will be told what you are to do." (Acts 9:3–6)

That was all it took and Paul became the greatest apostle there ever was. On what basis, then, do you doubt that the exalted Christ can make use of your life, deliver you from your sins, change your heart and mind and life? He will certainly do so, according to his own particular plan and purpose for you, if you are joined to him by faith.

Paul also provides another example of the power available to us through Christ. He writes of receiving a thorn in his flesh, "a messenger of Satan to harass me" (2 Cor. 12:7). He couldn't stand it. He couldn't take it any longer, whatever it was. Three times he pleaded for the Lord to take the thorn away. But God did not take it away. Instead, he gave Paul power to endure it cheerfully. God said, "My grace is sufficient for you, for my power is made perfect in weakness" (v. 9). Paul, who earlier had complained that his thorn was unbearable, replied, "Therefore I will boast all the more gladly of my weaknesses, so that the power of Christ may rest upon me. For the sake of Christ, then, I am content with weaknesses, insults, hardships, persecutions, and calamities. For when I am weak, then I am strong" (vv. 9–10).

We think that Christ's power has let us down or is disproved if we have any troubles, any temptations, any weaknesses that have not been removed. But Paul says that Christ's power enables us to endure in them by faith so that he may be glorified in our weakness. Martyn Lloyd-Jones observes:

> As we contemplate life and all its difficulties, and as we are tempted by Satan to feel that all is impossible, and that we cannot go on because we are so weak and the difficulties so baffling, we must remind ourselves of this truth and say: I am a very small and unimportant member, but I am a member of the body of Christ; I am "in him," and therefore, whatever may be true of me personally, the life of the Head is in me . . . I am in touch with Him, His vital energy is in me . . . As our eyes are opened to this truth we can take fresh courage, and take up our task again and say: In Christ I cannot fail, I must not fail, He will not allow me to fail.[1]

The third application has to do especially with the church. People don't think much of the church, even Christians. The church is somewhere they go to get something for themselves, to get a lift, to get some help, to make some decent friends. The world looks on the church as something insignificant and weak. The great things in this world deal with skyscrapers and stock markets, rising and falling empires. This way of thinking was especially a danger for the fledging churches of Paul's day; they were viewed, and might have viewed themselves, as an insignificant cult among a sea of religious groups. But here we see that the church cannot be rightly understood apart from seeing the exalted Christ, who rules over every power and all of history, and its relationship to him. *The church is the preeminent institution in all the world* because it is the body of him who is seated at God's right hand in the heavenly realms. Only the church, among all institutions, will endure, its accomplishments blazing forever when all else has passed away.

There is therefore no greater privilege than membership in the church. There is no greater calling than the Christian's calling to offer his gifts and talents, time and money to the work of the church. A Christian who gives all his energy to his job, or uses her talents only for personal gain, or spends his money all on himself, neglecting the work of the church, which will last forever, is simply a fool. Such a person does not recognize that the church is the body, the temple, the bride of him who is exalted on high. In the end it is what Christ has done through the church that will matter most, will most shine in glory, and will have been most worth the offering of our lives. Therefore a Christian who is not involved in a church's ministry, who does not pray regularly for the work of the church, who is taking but never giving to the church, should seriously ask if he really understands what this life is about, if she really sees this Christ who is exalted, and if so, what kind of response is appropriate to that faith.

The Church as the Fullness of Christ

Paul concludes with one of the most remarkable statements in all the New Testament. He describes the church as "the fullness of him who fills all in all" (Eph. 1:23).

There are two ways in which the church may be understood as "the fullness" of Christ, and scholars are divided on the issue. The first and most accepted view is that Paul means that the church is filled with and by Christ, "who fills everything in every way." The advantage of this view is that it fits with what we find elsewhere in the Bible. Andrew Lincoln explains, "Everywhere else Christ is portrayed as actively filling believers rather than being filled by them . . . [otherwise] a deficiency in his person would be implied."[2] Charles Hodge takes this view, explaining, "As the body is filled or pervaded by the soul, so the church is filled by the Spirit of Christ; or, as God of old dwelt in the temple, and filled it with his glory, so Christ now dwells in his church and fills it with his presence."[3]

All of that is true, but I think the second view better fits what Paul is saying here. Paul's writing here is very bold, and we should not shrink from being equally bold, understanding that the church fills Christ, even as Christ is the One who fills all in all.

In what sense, then, might we say that we are the fullness of Christ? It is of course true that, being God, the Lord Jesus is self-sufficient and does not need us or anything else. But as our Mediator and Redeemer, he is joined to the church as the head to the body and in that sense requires us to be complete. That is the straightforward meaning of Paul's words in this verse. First he names us the body to Christ's head and then designates the church as the fullness of him who fills all things. John Calvin therefore says:

> This is the highest honor of the Church, that, unless He is united to us, the Son of God reckons Himself in some measure imperfect. What an encouragement it is for us to hear, that, not until He has us as one with Himself, is He complete in all His parts, or does He wish to be regarded as whole![4]

That is the highest ground of our hope for salvation. Arthur Pink says, "There cannot be a Redeemer without redeemed, a Shepherd without sheep, a Bridegroom without a bride, a living Head without a living body. He is *her* fullness as the Lord of life and grace; she is *His* fullness since by means of the glory He has put upon her He will hereafter be magnified."[5] That being the case, we see why Christ so loves his church and why he secures for us a place where he is and provides for us his own power. Even this filling of himself is his own work, his own filling of all things in every way to the praise of his glorious grace. He says, "Because I live, you also will live" (John 14:19).

Here Comes the Bride

I want to conclude by reflecting on the glory that Christ will receive at the end of history by means of his union with the church. At the end, all creation will be regenerated in glory and will unite in his acclamation. Of him especially is it written, "The mountains and the hills before you shall break forth into singing, and all the trees of the field shall clap their hands" (Isa. 55:12). Furthermore, as the Book of Revelation so vividly depicts, the legions of angels will offer up their praise, with the "voice of a great multitude, like the roar of many waters, and like the sound of mighty peals of thunder," acclaiming the Lion who is a Lamb, the Lord Almighty who reigns forever (Rev. 19:6).

The Bible tells us that the scene at the consummation of all things is a wedding. The angels will rejoice: "Let us rejoice and exult and give him the glory, for the marriage of the Lamb has come, and his Bride has made herself ready" (Rev. 19:7). That is where we, the church, fit in, as the bride who is given to the groom, and who gives herself to him in the fullness of their love.

I have had the privilege of officiating at a great many weddings. A wedding is, of course, most festive—a time of beauty and joy. The church is always finely decorated, and as the minister in my robe I always try to look my best. But I have noticed one thing that is always true. When the doors open, and the bride is revealed, and as she begins her procession to join the groom who stands by my side for their entry into marital union, he only has eyes for her. Magnificent as the church may appear, resplendent as are all those in attendance, the groom's eyes are fixed on his bride alone. She beams at him with love, and hers is the adoration that fills his heart and lifts up his face in tears of joy.

That is the destiny of Christ and his church. And if that is how it will be at the end, when all the created realm is in attendance, worshiping the Savior and Lord in glory, imagine the pleasure our Lord and Head takes even now through the worship we give to him. Imagine how much it means to his heart as we, his betrothed bride, look forward even now to that great wedding day to come, as we look to him in love, and as we live our lives to the praise of his name. To him be glory, both now and forever.

NOTES

Preface

1. John Calvin, *Institutes of the Christian Religion,* ed. John T. McNeill, 2 vols. (Philadelphia: Westminster, 1960), 4.1.4.

Chapter 1: Prologue: "I Will Build My Church"

1. Michael Green, *The Message of Matthew: The Kingdom of Heaven* (Downers Grove, IL: InterVarsity, 2000), 177.

2. Ibid.

3. Ibid., 178.

4. Ibid., 179–80.

5. See James M. Boice, *Psalms,* 3 vols. (Grand Rapids: Baker, 1994), 1:101.

6. Mindy Belz, "We Have Nothing but We Have Everything," *World,* June 17, 2000, 46–48.

7. J. C. Ryle, *Light from Old Times* (Moscow, ID: Charles Nolan, 2000), 157.

8. Ibid., 158.

9. Thomas Kelly, "Stricken, Smitten, and Afflicted," 1804.

Chapter 2: One Church

1. Archbishop of Canterbury George Carey, *Sermon at Ecumenical Vespers, Anglican/Vatican Consultations,* 17 May 2000, www.archbishopof canterbury/carey/(accessed January 14, 2004).

2. Catholic Answers, "Pillar of Fire, Pillar of Truth," quoted in *Onward Christian Soldiers: Protestants Affirm the Church,* ed. Don Kistler (Morgan, PA: Soli Deo Gloria, 1999), 227.

3. Bruce Shelley, "Denominations—Divided We Stand," *Christianity Today,* September 7, 1998, 90.

4. D. Martyn Lloyd-Jones, *Growing in the Spirit: The Assurance of Our Salvation* (Wheaton, IL: Crossway, 1989), 138–40.

5. James M. Boice, *Acts: An Expositional Commentary* (Grand Rapids: Baker, 1998), 92.

6. R. C. Sproul, "One O'er All the Earth," in *Onward Christian Soldiers: Protestants Affirm the Church*, ed. Don Kistler (Morgan, PA: Soli Deo Gloria, 1999), 212–13.

7. Francis A. Schaeffer, *The Church at the End of the Twentieth Century*, from *The Complete Works of Francis Schaeffer: A Christian Worldview*, 5 vols. (Wheaton, IL: Crossway, 1982), 4:102.

8. Jeremiah Burroughs, *Gospel Conversation,* ed. Don Kistler (1648; reprint, Morgan, PA: Soli Deo Gloria, 1995), 150.

9. Paul F. M. Zahl, *Five Women of the English Reformation* (Grand Rapids: Eerdmans, 2001), 110–13.

10. Hal Hopson, "Though I May Speak with Bravest Fire," © 1972, Hope Publishing.

Chapter 3: A Holy Church

1. John Calvin, quoted in R. C. Sproul, *Faith Alone: The Evangelical Doctrine of Justification* (Grand Rapids: Baker, 1995), 102.

2. Edmund P. Clowney, *The Church,* Contours of Christian Theology (Downers Grove, IL: InterVarsity, 1995), 87.

3. Donald Grey Barnhouse, *Let Me Illustrate: Stories, Anecdotes, Illustrations* (Westwood, NJ: Fleming Revell, 1967), 196.

4. John Owen, quoted in Clowney, *The Church,* 88.

5. "Religion Is Gaining Ground, but Morality Is Losing Ground," *Emerging Trends,* 23:7 (September 2001), 1–2.

6. Jonathan Edwards, *Jonathan Edwards' Resolutions: And Advice to Young Converts,* ed. Stephen J. Nichols (Phillipsburg, NJ: P&R, 2001), Resolution 56.

7. Eric Alexander, "The Application of Redemption," in *To Glorify and Enjoy God: A Commemoration of the 350ᵗʰ Anniversary of the Westminster Assembly,* ed. John L. Carson and David W. Hall (Edinburgh: Banner of Truth, 1994), 245.

8. Ibid., 245–46.

Chapter 4: A Catholic Church

1. Paul F. Boller Jr., *Presidential Campaigns* (New York: Oxford University Press, 1984), 226.

2. Ibid., 229.

3. Henry Bettenson, ed., *The Early Christian Fathers: A Selection from the Writings of the Fathers from St. Clement to St. Athanasius* (New York: Oxford University Press, 1956), 247.

4. Cyril of Jerusalem, in his *Catechetical Lectures,* trans. E. W. Gifford, Nicene and Post-Nicene Fathers, Second Series, vol. 7 (reprint, Peabody, MA: Hendrickson, 1994), 139–40.

5. Ironically, in the modern period, the word "catholic" as an adjective has come to mean almost exactly the opposite—someone who doesn't draw distinctions, but tries to learn from the good in all.

6. Zacharias Ursinus, *The Commentary of Dr. Zacharias Ursinus on the Heidelberg Catechism,* trans. G. W. Williard (1852; reprint; Phillipsburg, NJ: P&R, 1985), 289–90.

7. James Bannerman, *The Church of Christ,* vol. 1 (1869; reprint, Edinburgh: Banner of Truth, 1960), 43–44.

8. John Bunyan, *Grace Abounding to the Chief of Sinners* (London: Oxford University Press, 1962), 229.

9. Charles Bridges, *The Christian Ministry* (Edinburgh: Banner of Truth, 1980), 1.

10. Two qualifications I would make to this call are divisions, first, for the purpose of language and, second, for the purpose of evangelism. Language is an inherent part of the Christian life. If preaching is to be central to the congregation's life, it should be understood. Therefore, organizing congregations around understood languages is necessary. Second, evangelistic outreaches can certainly focus on one particular subgroup in a culture. But those desiring to evangelize a group or community should be very careful not to distort the gospel with the churches they begin, the very churches that are intended by Christ to personify the gospel. Ephesians 2, Acts 6, and Revelation 7 are good chapters to consider carefully for some of the reasons and challenges of multiethnic congregations.

Chapter 5: An Apostolic Church

1. Edmund P. Clowney, *The Church,* Contours of Christian Theology (Downers Grove, IL: InterVarsity, 1995), 73.

2. James M. Boice, *Ephesians: An Expositional Commentary* (Grand Rapids: Baker, 1997), 91.

3. Andrew Hill, personal correspondence.

4. Clowney, *The Church,* 77.

5. Hans Kung, quoted in Clowney, *The Church,* 77.

6. Paul Althaus, *The Theology of Martin Luther,* trans. Robert C. Schultz (Philadelphia: Fortress, 1966), 5.

Chapter 6: Epilogue: Christ and His Church

1. D. Martyn Lloyd-Jones, *God's Ultimate Purpose: An Exposition of Ephesians 1:1–23* (Grand Rapids: Baker, 1978), 430.

2. Andrew T. Lincoln, *Ephesians* (Dallas, TX: Word, 1990), 75.

3. Charles Hodge, *A Commentary on Ephesians* (1856; reprint, Carlisle, PA: Banner of Truth, 1964), 54.

4. John Calvin, *The Epistles of Paul the Apostle to the Galatians, Ephesians, Philippians and Colossians* (Grand Rapids: Eerdmans, 1965), 138.

5. Arthur Pink, *The Ability of God: Prayers of the Apostle Paul* (Chicago: Moody, 2000), 217.

Index of Scripture

2:5—48
2:6-7—97
2:9—48
2:22-23—43

2 Peter
3:2—105

1 John
1:7—56
3:3—56

Jude
3—33

4—33
22-23—38

Revelation
19:6—131
19:7—131

INDEX OF SUBJECTS
AND NAMES

141

Richard D. Phillips (M.Div., Westminster Theological Seminary) is the senior minister of First Presbyterian Church of Coral Springs in Margate, Florida. Phillips is also director of the Philadelphia Conference on Reformation Theology. His numerous books include *Turning Back the Darkness* and *Chosen in Christ*.

Philip G. Ryken (M.Div., Westminster Theological Seminary; D.Phil., University of Oxford) is senior minister of Tenth Presbyterian Church in Philadelphia. He serves on the council of the Alliance of Confessing Evangelicals. His published work includes *The Heart of the Cross* (with James Montgomery Boice), *Jeremiah and Lamentations, The Doctrines of Grace* (with Boice), *The Message of Salvation,* and *My Father's World*.

Mark E. Dever (M.Div., Gordon-Conwell Theological Seminary; Th.D., Southern Baptist Theological Seminary; Ph.D., Cambridge University, as J. B. Lightfoot scholar) is senior pastor of Capitol Hill Baptist Church in Washington, D.C., and has taught for the faculty of divinity at Cambridge University. He is also the senior fellow for the Center for Church Reform in Washington and speaks internationally at pastors' conferences and campus ministries. He is author of *Nine Marks of a Healthy Church*.